SPOILED
FOR
CHOICE

FOOD SCARES UNSCRAMBLED

QUENTIN SEDDON

EVERGREEN PUBLISHING LIMITED

Evergreen Publishing Limited was formed to fill a need within the specialist, technical fields of agriculture, food and biotechnology.

Spoiled for Choice is the first publication by Evergreen Publishing, but its founders, Christopher and David Green, have been involved in the agriculture and food industry for many years.

SPOILED
FOR
CHOICE

FOOD SCARES UNSCRAMBLED

QUENTIN SEDDON

Evergreen Publishing Limited
Stag House
The Hopgrounds
Finchingfield
Essex CM7 4LU

First published 1990

Evergreen Publishing Ltd
Stag House
The Hopgrounds
Finchingfield
Essex
CM7 4LU

© 1990

ISBN No. 0 9515898 0 6
A CIP catalogue record for this book is available from the British Library

Typeset in Baskerville

Cover design by Green Resources Limited and Cambridge Marketing Limited
Printed in Great Britain

QUENTIN SEDDON

Quentin Seddon was educated at schools in England and Australia before reading history at Oxford. He then worked for ten years for the publishers Longmans in London, Africa and Australia, before starting to farm in Devon in the early 1970s.

Towards the end of that decade he began to write about farming, and since then has been published in the *Guardian* as well as the *Farmers Weekly*, *The Field* and the *Countryside Commission News*. He has also broadcast on a regular basis for the BBC on farming matters for both radio and television.

As a result of an involvement with BBC Pebble Mill in producing documentary programmes marking the Year of Food and Farming 1989, his book, *The Silent Revolution*, telling the story of the post-war farming revolution, was published by BBC Enterprises.

While continuing to fulfill various other journalistic tasks, Quentin Seddon is the publisher of the agricultural markets' and commodities newsletter, *Farm Brief.*

AUTHOR'S ACKNOWLEDGEMENTS

I gratefully acknowledge the very valuable contributions given to me by so many individuals and organisations in researching this book.

It is difficult to list all, but many will readily recognise their contributions and I thank them for sharing this information which has enabled me to write *Spoiled for Choice*.

Geoffrey Cannon - *Politics of Food*; Frederick Accum - *There is Death in the Pot*; John Postgate - *Microbes and Man*; Michael Leathes and Martin Terry - *The Hormone Scandal*; Dr Jonathan Brostoff and Linda Gamlin - *Food Allergy and Intolerance*; Edith Efron - *The Apocalyptics*; David Goodman, Bernardo Sorj and John Wilkinson - *From Farming to Biotechnology*; Professor Philip James - *Healthy Nutrition*; Rachel Carson - *Silent Spring*; Ralph Nader - *Unsafe At Any Speed*; T. L. Cleave, G. D. Campbell, N. S. Painter - *Diabetes, Coronary Thrombosis and the Saccharin Disease*; Audrey Eyton - *The F-Plan Diet*.

Baroness Oppenheim-Barnes; James Lovelock; Sir Jack Drummond; Dr Roger Whitehead; Dr Mike Rayner; Ralph Blanchfield; Dr Verner Wheelock; Daphne Grose; Diane Roberts; Sir Donald Acheson; Dr Barbara Lund; Richard North; Gwyn Ashton; Professor Bourne; Keith Meldrum; Dr Eileen Rubery; Dr Klaus Gerigk; Dr Tom Crossett; Professor Barbara Clayton; Joy Wingfield; H. Carter; Professor Richard Lacey; Maurice Hanssen; Harold McGee; Dr Tom Coultate; Dr Ben Feingold; Professor Will Waites; Dr Roger Fenwick; Dr V. O. Wodicka; Professor Sir Richard Doll; Richard Peto; Peter Hutt; Richard Merrill; Professor Ames; Helen Blackholly; Paul Thomas; Professor Geoffrey Campbell-Platt; Dr Bevan Moseley; Rachel Waterhouse; Congressman Peter Smith; Dr Frank Raymond; Agner Niemann-Sorensen; Jeremy Rifkin; Samuel Epstein; Walter Beswick; Dr Roger Straughan; Mark Cantley; David Maclean; Sir Robert McCarrison; Dr I. Johnson; Sir Mark Richmond.

Spoiled for Choice

CONTENTS

ABBREVIATIONS

ACINF	Advisory Committee on Irradiated and Novel Foods
AFRC	Agricultural and Food Research Council
BMA	British Medical Association
BVA	British Veterinary Association
CA	Consumers' Association
CECG	Consumers in the European Community Group
DoH	Department of Health
DTI	Department of Trade and Industry
EPA	Environmental Protection Agency
FAC	Food Advisory Committee
FACT	Food Additives Campaign Team
FAO	Food and Agriculture Organisation
FDA	Food and Drug Administration
FDF	Food and Drink Federation
HSC	Health and Safety Commission
IFR	Institute of Food Research
LFC	London Food Commission
MAFF	Ministry of Agriculture, Fisheries and Food
NCC	National Consumers' Council
NOAH	National Office of Animal Health
PHLS	Public Health Laboratory Service
SCF	Scientific Committee for Food
WHO	World Health Organisation

Should you be frightened of food? No, is the answer this book gives. It accepts that there are, as there have always been, risks and pinpoints the ones which have become worse as well as the many others which have been over-emphasised and distorted.

Eggs and poultry, hazelnut yoghurt and soft cheeses, beansprouts and apples, beef and pâté, tap water and bottled water are just some of the things which have hit the headlines. When they did, sales and confidence crashed and common sense very often followed. It got to the point by the end of the year that market research showed three out of four of us no longer knew whom, or what, to believe about the food we eat.

Scares like this were greatly boosted when farming started to produce surpluses. For the first time in history we could pick and choose. This welcome luxury saw equally welcome demands for higher standards. Those will and should continue, but not at the expense of unbalanced criticism which creates unnecessary anxiety and wastes time and money which could be much better spent elsewhere.

The main message of this book is that those of us who have been afflicted by the recent diet of media food scares have less to worry about than we may have feared. Take eggs. Did they cause much of the food poisoning twelve months ago? If so, there should be fewer people ill today.

Eggs have been checked and double checked for infection; flocks of suspect chickens have been killed; and we are eating fewer eggs than we used to. If they were to blame, what's happened since should mean less food poisoning. But in the first three months of 1990 reported cases were rising even faster than they were a year ago.

We need to know what's happening, where the real risks lie and where they have been blown up to cause needless anxiety. The author looks closely at a number of these issues, describes the arguments and helps you to assess the facts behind the headlines. In doing so, he has written a book which brings much-needed balance back into the food debate.

Lord Plumb of Coleshill DL MEP
Former President of the European Parliament

CHAPTER ONE:
Introduction

There is a butcher in Nottinghamshire who meets a steady demand for 25kg to 30kg lambs. He cannot buy them in the markets, which today supply lambs in the range from 17kg to 23kg. The heavy lambs he needs are of the very fat type we have revelled in for hundreds of years but now reject as unhealthy and he has to make special arrangements with a local farmer to be sure of getting them. His customers are the miners in the Nottinghamshire coalfield and at the end of a shift they do not want a morsel of lean, underdone lamb with a whiff of garlic and rosemary. They want enormous, glistening shoulders, large well-cooked chops and great fat legs to replace the energy they have burned off mining coal.

Fifty years ago there were more than a million miners who would have liked good fat lamb to eat – though as George Orwell pointed out, what they mostly ate was white bread and margarine, corned beef, sugared tea and potatoes – and many of the rest of us worked more like miners too, which is why the sinews of a healthy diet were eggs, butter, cheese, milk and meat. They still are for hard-working people. The difference is not in the foods but in us. Today for many of us such a diet would not lead to more coal but more cholesterol and what we eat has hugely changed in consequence.

This has provoked a row. Some, like Baroness Oppen-heim-Barnes, now retired from the National Consumer Council, have said that 'the British consumer is served by probably the best food industry in the world with a wide choice of ever more sophisticated prepared and fresh foods available at reasonable cost retailed and pro-duced for the most part expertly and well.' Others, like Geoffrey Cannon in his book *The Politics of Food* say that 'British food is just about the worst in the Western world.'

Supporters of the food industry back the often tech-nically-driven changes thrown up by the competitive, profit-related demands of the market place. Critics assert that consumers are exploited by a profiteering combine of business and government and recoil from food technology – as if bread, wine, beer, cheese, choco-late or a baked potato were not the products of various technologies.

The row is interesting and important. Consumers, served or exploited, are getting power. The more pow-erful they get the more they are subject to manipulation. There is the manipulation by advertising and the mar-keteers who must please their masters by keeping food sales moving. There is manipulation by interest groups. There is manipulation by the media. There is manipu-lation by politicians, for although food has always been a political commodity it has now become a matter of party politics, and all too often petty party politics.

It seems likely that the changes which have so quickly cut the numbers of miners to under 100,000 will con-tinue to accelerate new working patterns, new life styles, new personal habits – and new foods and new technolo-gies to go with them. The power of consumers now demands that the industry which supplies their food works more closely with them to match the patterns and possibilities of the future. That in turn demands judgment about what really counts and what can be safely ignored.

We have recently been warned of the dangers of getting this wrong – and by no one more clearly than James Lovelock, grandfather to the Greens. Best-known today for his idea of Gaia, that the earth is a living organism whose balance and well-being is sustained by life itself, Lovelock's Green grandpaternity goes back to the invention of the electron capture detector. He has described the origins of that device in the early 1950s.

'I well remember buying dusty war surplus electronics gear from shops in Lisle Street, near Leicester Square. Shops that existed in juxtaposition with massage parlours and displays of libidinous literature. I often wondered how the girls that roamed the streets knew so unerringly who of us were their potential customers. They never confused those in search of electronics with those in search of erotics. It was with the bits and pieces from Lisle Street that I made in 1957 my first electron capture detector, the device that was destined to provide the data that enabled Rachel Carson to write *Silent Spring* and which first discovered the CFCs in the atmosphere.'

In the late autumn of 1988, Lovelock gave the annual Schumaker lecture in Bristol. Of the electron capture detector he said, 'it is still the most sensitive, easily portable and inexpensive analytical device in existence today. It is so exquisitely sensitive that if a few litres of a certain perfluorocarbon were allowed to evaporate somewhere in Japan we could easily detect it in the atmosphere here in Bristol a few days later, and within a year or so it would be detectable anywhere in the world . . .

'The discovery of the ubiquitous distribution of measurable, but usually trivial, quantities of pesticides and numerous other chemicals by the electron capture detector, opened a niche for the environmental industry . . . The general public found in this new environmentalism a way to express their fears of things scientific and technological. There was an amazing collection of scapegoats for them to blame for their personal and collective ills. Not for one moment would I suggest that there was a conspiracy, there was no need for one . . .

'Do not take what I say to mean that I regard as unimportant the presence in the environment of radiation and chemicals at levels that could cause a significant increase in cancer. What I am saying is that given the exquisite sensitivity of the instruments it is all too easy to find carcinogens everywhere, even when the danger from them is very small . . . Before I invented the device it would have been quite easy and reasonable to set zero as the lower permissible limit of pesticide residues in foodstuffs. In practice, zero really means the least that can be detected and after the electron capture detector appeared, zero as a limit became so low that to apply it would have caused the rejection of nearly everything that was edible; even organically grown vegetables contain measurable levels of pesticides, so sensitive is the device.

'What was needed was common sense and the acceptance of the wisdom of the physician Paracelsus who said long ago, "The poison is the dose".'

A year later, when Lovelock gave the John Preedy Memorial Lecture to the Friends of the Earth, he came back to a similar theme with fresh vigour. He began by reflecting on a time of difficulty before he had equipped environmentalism with the electron capture detector. 'In 1938 we all knew that war was inevitable, what we did not know was when it would come and what would happen when it did. Like now there was a great deal of confusion over what to do. Many in those days thought Hitler to be a lesser threat than Stalin.

'Today we face a different, but just as certain threat,

environmental disorder. Just as in 1939 there were confused voices calling for contradictory action, so there are now. There are those who see the environment in human terms only and seem to regard the science-based chemical and nuclear industries as the only enemy. Their behaviour is as inconsistent and as negative as that of those of the left who after Munich called stridently for disarmament. Others see the preservation of wild life, particularly cuddly animals and rare birds as the main if not the only problem. They are limited in their vision like those of the right who saw Russia as the only threat. It took the invasion of Bohemia and of Poland to make it clear who was the enemy and what was the real cause. I suspect that it will take the first great surprises soon to come to awaken us as did war 50 years ago . . .

'Most of us are hypochondriacs in one way or another and are vulnerable to the pleas of those scientists who ask us to call for legislation against some chemical or radiation in the environment. Such pleas are especially seductive when they tell us that there is a danger of cancer. Nothing so frightens the average person as the thought of death by that painful and degrading disease. I think that few actions are more despicable than the manipulation of this fear by corrupt scientists for their short term personal advantage . . .

'The multinationals have for years been the only human agencies to take a long-term, 20 year look, into the future. They have to. What profit would they make in a world devoid of customers? . . . Sometimes the response of the scientists in the multinationals is the only one we have . . . It won't be some cottage industry that makes the alternative safe refrigerants, it will be the multinational chemical industry.'

Lovelock's call is for the wise use of science and technology to save both humans and the planet. He has even suggested that industry should be encouraged to synthesise all our food so that we can give the land we use for farming back to Gaia. No doubt he teases: Gaia herself can hardly resent the regime of mowing and extensive grazing which created traditional hay meadows – although, in striking contrast, the intensive organic horticulture which Chinese farmers have sustained successfully over 40 centuries leaves little enough room for wildlife.

In making such suggestions, Lovelock argues against those who believe passionately that science, technology and industry are the simple cause, rather than the potential cure, of our problems. He has a lot of people to convince, for these passionate beliefs are far earlier than the origins of his belief in Gaia. Here is a forceful example.

'Hospitals are filled with a thousand screaming victims; the palaces of luxury and the hovels of indigence resound alike with the bitter wailings of disease; idiotism and madness grin and rave among us, and all these complicated calamities result from those unnatural habits of life to which the human race has addicted itself . . .' This was Shelley, writing early in the nineteenth century, and the unnatural habits he savaged were the food and drink of his contemporaries. He held commerce – 'with all its vices, selfishness and corruption . . . a foe of everything of real worth and excellence in the human character' – largely responsible.

The poet might, with considerable justification, play on the emotions. Foreshadowing Lovelock's arguments, it was science which would begin to clear up the mess. Everybody knew that food was adulterated but the food laws which went back to the thirteenth century were impossible to enforce unless the guilty were caught in the act. The change came with the slow advance of analytic chemistry, and the first blast of this change was released by Frederick Accum in 1820 – very close to the date when Shelley was writing – who published a book whose subtitle, *There is Death in the Pot*, excellently summarised the tale he had to tell.

Accum, who had worked with Sir Humphrey Davy, was a professor of Chemistry whose work over many years made clear that much food and drink was adulterated; not only did he describe the tricks of the hucksters' trade, he also named the hucksters. The historian of food John Burnett quotes a contemporary source which, after Accum, lamented: 'Bread turns out to be a crutch to help us onward to the grave, instead of the staff of life; in porter there is no support, in cordials no consolation, in almost everything poison, and in scarcely any medicine cure.'

It was thus to take Accum and others 40 years before the Adulteration of Food Act of 1860 made the first attempt to turn hucksters into criminals, but Burnett describes it as a total failure. It did, however, lead to the Sale of Food and Drugs Act 15 years later which saw the beginnings of an improvement in food purity. When that Act was passed, one in five samples of food and drink – and one in two of bread – tested by public analysts were contaminated. As late as 1913 this remained true for one sample in twelve analysed; by then bread was almost never adulterated, though beer and spirits, coffee and milk were frequent culprits. The chief contaminant was added water. Deliberate and dangerous adulteration had become very infrequent.

Although Accum's book exposed these and many other scandals, and although it was followed by titles like *Disease and Death in the Pot and Bottle* and, more solemnly, a *Treatise on the Falsifications of Food*, little happened to improve the people's vittles. In part this was inertia, in part dogma; for the laissez-faire economic theories of Adam Smith persuaded governments that they should not intervene. Such attitudes saw the Assize of Bread – which had controlled the price and quality of a loaf for 550 years – repealed in 1815, and the Corn Laws repealed in 1846. Smith's economic arguments entered the political arena in the violent conflict between old landowning and new commercial and industrial money over where the nation should grow its food and how much it should pay for it. The Repeal of the Corn Laws settled the debate when it opened British farming to free trade and British workmen to the ambiguous joys of cheap food. The influence of this victory was to last for more than a century until it ended in an egg, sausage, chips and beans cul-de-sac. Consumers and the food industry who between them are finally ditching 150 years devoted to cheap food and quantity for wide-ranging choice and quality are much helped by the fact that modern technology has made food cheaper now than ever before.

Echoes of these old battles ring loud enough for some of today's contestants to join Shelley in pitching the struggle still between good and evil. This book argues in support of Lovelock's pleas for judgment and balance. It sets the scene by looking briefly at the history of food demand and supply over the last 100 years. After that it concentrates on recent food scares and future food worries – and the question it tries to answer as it analyses these events is, how worried about food should we be?

CHAPTER TWO:

Food Demand from Queen to Commoner

Queen Victoria kept an indoor staff of over 300 at Windsor and a kitchen staff of 45 to serve her food, and what the Queen kept the gentry copied according to their means. Some of the aristocracy matched or exceeded Her Majesty, but even modest middle class families of two parents and three children kept five more folk in their household to serve them.

Towards the end of the Queen's reign, the Victorian dinner party became a major form of social expression and prestige, so that when looked at now the length and richness of typical menus have become incomprehensible. These habits lasted into Edwardian times, when a craze developed for rare and out-of-season foods to enhance the status of the host. They were to percolate slowly through society until they reappeared much more widely in the 1960s when dinner parties again strove for novelty, theatricality and entertainment – qualities still commonly pursued today with the continuing growth of the chattering classes and now beginning to be offered to mass markets through the superstores.

Meanwhile poor people went often ill-fed and always worse nourished. Anyone over five feet tall was acceptable to the generals preparing to fight the Boers in 1899, but it wasn't easy to find enough soldiers. Two out of five possible recruits were so feeble they had to be rejected. The government of the day may have been indifferent to the personal health of its citizens; there was cause to worry if national security was to depend on an army of crippled dwarves. But it was to be left to the reforming Liberal government of 1906 to try to improve the nation's health by introducing free school meals, at least for some children.

Burnett quotes the nutritionist Sir Jack Drummond's statement that 'the opening of the twentieth century saw malnutrition more rife in England than it had been since the great dearths of medieval and Tudor times' only to claim that it is almost certainly untrue. 'Investigation was revealing for the first time the extent and effects of underfeeding, but appalling as these were, they would have been found greater still in the middle of the nineteenth century if anyone had cared to look or had known what to look for.'

Whatever the truth, improvement was slow. When men were needed to confront the Kaiser in 1914, two out of five were still too feeble to fight. 'Of every nine men of military age in Great Britain, on the average three were perfect, fit, and healthy; two were on a definitely inferior plane of health and strength, whether from some disability or some failure of development; three were incapable of undergoing more than a very moderate degree of physical exertion, and could almost (in view of their age) be described with justice as physical wrecks; and the remaining man was a chronic invalid with a precarious hold on life.'

By 1935, the dreadful state of health of young men of military age had worsened, and two out of three volunteers failed to achieve the low standard of physique which the army needed. In 1936 *The Times* reported John Boyd Orr's finding that 'one-half of the population is living on a diet insufficient or ill-designed to maintain health'. This famous piece of research continued to echo round the diet debate for many years. Boyd Orr advised that poor people needed much more food of animal origin, particularly milk and dairy products, than they got. His influence sustained the virtues of these foods for over 40 years, until advice in the early 1980s switched to recommending less animal fat. Many have disputed Orr's claims about the extent of malnutrition, but in the context of the hungry 1930s his arguments were irresistible.

Inevitably, his recommendations were rapidly politicised. The Jarrow march saw Labour MP Tim Johnston using Boyd Orr's evidence to attack the government. The use of nutritional evidence – often open to differing interpretations – to bash the government of the day which Johnston employed then has remained a weapon in the party political armoury.

Boyd Orr and his critics could soon point to improvement in the fitness of army recruits. Two out of three of the men called up to fight Hitler in 1939 were physically able to do so, and from then on fears for the national physique have declined. For the first time in a long while the horrifying gap between the health and well-being of rich and poor shrank to insignificance and we paraded as a nation fit to fight.

The fact that this fundamental achievement came from intelligent organisation of supply rather than free market changes in demand has not been lost on those who now argue for increasing controls over food supplies.

Other assessments confirm these improvements in our health. Dr Roger Whitehead, director of the Dunn Nutrition Laboratory in Cambridge, has scanned the records of children's height. Over most of the last 100 years the height of five year olds has been increasing, and other physical measures show how we have expanded physically. In terms of basic health, he says, this means our food is far better than it used to be.

The improvement is mainly because we are richer. Wealth has meant changing demand, with many more consumers who expect to live like Edwardian aristocrats. Out-of-season melons or grapes and fresh meat or dairy produce are delivered daily from the country estate to the modern equivalent of the kitchen door – the nearest supermarket. Housewives demand a wide variety of raw, processed and cooked foods constantly and easily available by once-a-week one-stop shopping. As much as anything, they demand convenience, so that sales of prepared, oven-ready, heat-and-eat or TV-dinner style foods increase year by year, while sales of snack foods match or outrun them.

Women spend less time shopping and less time cooking, especially as more of them go out to work, and more single parent homes see fewer sit-down family meals. The market researchers tell us that during the 1980s there have been fewer housewives and they have cooked fewer meals. No more than one house in 20 – about one million out of the total 21 million households – has Dad going out to work and Mum at home looking after the kids. There are nine million houses with two parents living together with their children, but in nearly five million of these where the kids are still young (under 15) their mothers go out to work. A further five million homes house single people, and the average size of a household today is just on two and a half people. Three-quarters of them have a deep freeze or fridge freezer, and getting on for half own microwave ovens.

Put all this together and less than one house in three still sees families sitting down together to eat a meal cooked in the kitchen by Mum. A recently published report suggested that 'kitchens will never be redundant but they are possibly closer to becoming mini-cafeterias, providing a series of meals at different times to suit the various members of the family.' Working mothers, single parents and single person households increasingly demand the convenience which comes when commercial kitchens do most of the peeling, chopping and cooking for them.

These trends have gone furthest in America. *The Wall Street Journal* reckons that the popularity of the microwave has more to do with racing than cooking. Americans apparently believe that eating has now become a pit-stop activity. Brillat-Savarin's observation, tell me what you eat and I will tell you who you are, now needs the answer, a sportscar. This may be less new than the *Journal* imagines. Food manufacturers have long split societies into those which want fuelling and those which want pleasing, and Americans have always led the refuelling convoy. They now claim that even fast food joints seem slow – because there are no queues in front of the family microwave. This urge to rush slows as it spreads across the Atlantic, but even in our own more somnolent culture children are to be seen standing in front of the toaster shouting 'Faster, faster'. Cooking is out and speed is in.

At the same time, natural foods are also popular. Sales of organically-grown food are rising fast, and supporters of that energetic movement say that the actual demand is much higher and simply cannot at present be met. No artificial flavourings, colourings or preservatives are claims frequently printed on food packaging, and these attitudes to additives also extend to natural preservatives like salt and vinegar.

They do not necessarily add to food safety. Unpasteurised milk is more natural than pasteurised, but more than four-fifths of the outbreaks of milk-borne food poisoning come from the 3% of milk sold unpasteurised. The move away to fewer, lighter or no preservation methods at the very least demands that the food chain must handle the resulting product with much greater speed and care.

Many of these changes are superficial. Changing basic

eating patterns is a slow business. Those who argue that we are eating less meat, for example, are right – so long as they stay at home. Add eating out, and we are swallowing more than ever, very nearly half a pound a head every day. Ten years ago, before fat scares were fully fanned, just under one-third of a pound of fat slid down daily. It still does. Some of it comes from the 23 million packets of crisps and savoury snacks we eat every day, some again from the half pound of chips we eat each week. More of this oily ooze comes from plants like maize, soya or sunflower and less from animals but the total amount we swallow is falling only slowly.

We are just as salty as we always were, and as for fibre the amount which goes down daily is yards less than it should be, no more than two-thirds the amount recommended by the World Health Organisation (WHO). And, while it is tough to tot up the grains of sugar, we are certainly eating more cakes, biscuits, shop-bought desserts and ice-cream than we did a few years back. We are also eating more fresh fruit and vegetables.

In short, our food demands are contradictory. As Dr Mike Rayner of the Coronary Prevention Group sums it up, while food eaten at home is a little bit healthier, this is more than offset by worrying trends in food eaten out.

By the end of the 1980s, £1 in every £4 which went on food and drink was spent out of the home, a total of close on £20 billion – and of the £12 billion which went on food alone, somewhere around £3 billion shot through the fast food chains. But accurate information on who eats what when eating out is not readily available, which adds to the difficulty of knowing how well fed we are. Burnett points out that National Food Survey Reports published every year since 1949 show the nation as a whole is well-nourished, but this tells us only about what we eat at home, and then only as an average. It is very clear that some of us remain malnourished.

'Family size has emerged as one of the chief determinants of nutritional adequacy and in families with two adults and four or more children there are downward gradients for almost all nutrients . . . The optimism about general standards of well-being of the population has also been shaken by the re-emergence of a problem of poverty in Britain . . . The Child Poverty Action Group has recently produced statistics which suggest an alarming increase . . Whatever the precise numbers of the poor there can now be little doubt that there are large groups in the population who are either in poverty or on the edge of it for whom marginal changes in income or a sudden crisis such as illness, death, or unemployment, can produce severe consequences. Evidence suggests that in such crises people tend to cut expenditure on food and drink rather than on fixed expenses such as rent, fuel, and hire-purchase payments.'

While teenagers who eat too much sweet and fatty food may end up malnourished, at least they are a declining proportion of the population. More worrying for the future are people on state pensions whose diets are restricted by shortage of cash. As they increase in numbers we could be faced with more, not less, malnutrition in Britain.

FOOD SUPPLY FROM EMPIRE TO COMMON MARKET

The industries supplying our food have struggled with these increasingly rapid changes in what, when and where we eat. If they often seem to lead, there is also a long tradition of following the market. When Shelley and Accum took their very different approaches to the problems of adulteration, nearly all processing and preservation were traditional technologies carried out on the farm or in the home. Supply and demand held hands with long-established eating habits. Costs of storage and transport were very low and choice was very limited. Large numbers of farmers sold through markets to large numbers of retailers who did any further processing, such as making pies. Effectively, retailers were thus the point in the industry where contamination was most likely to occur.

Industrialisation, the growth of population, the move from country to city and greater wealth, all led to revolutionary change in domestic food production, the food industry and food trade.

The rapid increase in numbers alone would have had this effect. Between 1750 and 1950 the population rose tenfold and most people moved to live in cities. To supply their food meant new ways of growing it but, much more, new ways of storing, transporting, manufacturing and selling it. The need to supply the cities forced unavoidable changes on the food industry.

The Empire was as important. Early this century we imported nearly all our bread flour, fats and sugar, three-quarters of our fruit and cheese and more than half our meat – and large firms were best placed to bring in this cheap food. Their size also helped them exploit new processing technology. Wholesalers, manufacturers and retailers all grew bigger and the battles between them more fierce. Each at different stages has come close to dominating the whole of the food industry.

Food supply today, a product of this history, is described as a mature industry – a jargon phrase which means it is no longer growing. The result is that profits no longer come from increased demand for goods. Instead, they come from innovation and competition. At the same time, because we spend a smaller proportion of our income on food as time passes, so the earnings of the food industry fall compared to national income as a whole. The squeeze on both income and profits thus compels increased efficiency, larger size – and added value. This bit of jargon means producing something in a new or different way which people pay more for. In adding cash value to its products industry is often accused of subtracting health or nutrition value. The truth in this charge is closely bound up with consumer behaviour. Potato crisps are a good example.

We began by importing them from France. Early this century they started to be made by local manufacturers and sales expanded. At much the same time the fashion for Health Food shops started, catching crisps in a battle between the Good Life and the market place. Crisps won. And, if that was still a time when the British thought healthy eating a masochistic folly best left to cranks, they still seem to be winning. Home-cooked potatoes are a healthy and nourishing food which cost between £50 and £150 a tonne at the farm gate. Crisps, full of fat and so criticised as unhealthy, can cost up to 100 times as much when we eat them. But we keep crunching. A mature industry would need to be fully staffed by saints to stop making and selling crisps, so the only way to cut the crunching is for consumers to buy fewer packets.

There are plenty of examples like crisps, but the main value added in recent years has come from service or convenience. If the food of Edwardian aristocrats came from a kitchen full of servants, today's version comes to us ready-wrapped from the manufacturers. Convenience foods have increasingly taken over food markets in the past 30 years, starting with cans and going right through to the new technologies of cook-chill and sous vide. This trend has also been attacked – for the way it uses additives, more expensive packaging, higher energy costs and safety risks, among other things. But in a mature market, adding value through service is inevitable so long as demand for the products continues – and once again those demands for service and convenience have been growing.

The skills of marketing backed these trends by pre-packaging, branding and advertising, which also boosted market concentration. Convenience and concentration became self-reinforcing because the costs of the first pushed businesses towards the second – and then pushed them back again towards the first since that was where the best returns lay. The results affected bread and marma-lade, cereals and eggs, soups and ice-creams. They explain why many different market sectors are now dominated by fewer than five businesses – including flour, bread, bis-cuits, breakfast foods, chocolate, soups, dairy products, margarine and many other goods – why half what we eat now comes from ten giant manufacturing companies, and why among them over the last 50 years technology has grown in importance.

Food science and food technology may have had their roots in the nineteenth century but they are very largely developments of the last 50 years. Their earliest fumblings affected some unusual people. Thus towards the turn of the century Sir George Sitwell, father of Edith, Osbert and Sacheverell, invented an artificial egg. The yolk was to be made of smoked meat, the white of compressed rice and the shell was of lime. He thought the egg, which could be stored indefinitely and eaten after brief boiling, would greatly ease the hunger of distant explorers. Osbert sug-gested that his father should patent the idea and that the right authority for advice on marketing the explorer's egg was Sir Gordon Selfridge. Only Sir George and Sir Gor-don know what happened in the course of their meeting, but when Sir George came home he put away his plans and diagrams and never mentioned his egg again.

Many new foods have suffered a similar fate. Mean-while, technology has advanced as the demands of large-scale food production confronted the industry with big-ger and bigger problems and firms struggled to control raw materials, quality and costs. Frozen foods are a good early example of quite a simple technology, where heavy capital and marketing costs meant that only the heavies could go in. Complications have increased since then and now embrace such varied areas as 'water-binding and fat-binding properties of meat; electron microscopy research into tissues of fruit, vegetables, meat and fish, and generally into the fine structures of foodstuffs and composite food systems; the behaviour and interaction of hydrocolloid gel systems; the interaction in processes combining two or more food preservation systems; studies in the nature and behaviour of food emulsions; studies in the nature and behaviour of food powders; fundamental studies on extrusion cooking of foods; research into enzymes responsible for deteriorative reactions in food, and improved means of inactivating them or inhibiting their effects; conversely, research into enzymes capable of causing desirable processes in food manufacture; studies in the area of intermediate moisture preservation; and, longer-term perhaps, the search for new methods of preservation, and the use of "genetic engineering" to produce new food materials.'

The list, part of this continuing process of innovation, comes from Ralph Blanchfield, a past President of the Institute of Food Science and Technology. He has also pointed out, for example, that starch to the food industry is no longer just starch. Once it was potato or wheat or sago. Now starch provides 'a specific set of functional properties and performance, such as cold-water solubility, or modified viscosity, or viscosity without detectable gel-structure, or delayed-action viscosity development, or freeze-thaw stability, or mouth-feel varying from very smooth to noticeably granular.' Food extrusion, the basis for an enormous snack industry, spinning and steam-texturising, fluidised beds, and ultra-high temperature processing and aseptic packaging have all been added to the armoury.

These technologies are easily installed by large businesses with highly-qualified staff and ready access to capital – who can also more easily meet rising standards demanded of hygiene, or of effluent control or other environmental regulations. So the trend to size will continue. By 2000, these companies will almost certainly be fewer and bigger still.

There have always been large numbers of small firms in the industry as well. Some 5000 firms work at food and drink manufacturing, and there are nearly 40,000 in distribution, and a growing minority of people believe that we would be better served by a much smaller, more regional industry. Although that will undoubtedly grow it will be hard put to match the momentum built up by the forces of supply and demand over the last 250 years which have led to the rise of the giants. Today, some three out of every four giant European food companies are British.

The same influences affected shops. In 1869 John James Sainsbury kept a dairy in Drury Lane. In 1882 he opened the first purpose-designed Sainsbury shop in Croydon. By 1914 there were 114 of them, and over twice as many in 1939. In July 1950 the first Sainsbury's self-service store opened in Croydon to begin the long march of the multiples, which moved up to double time when postwar building controls were relaxed in the 1950s.

Another acceleration came with the ending of resale price maintenance in 1964. This stopped manufacturers from fixing shop prices and saw 'pile it high and sell it cheap' drive into retailing – and drive out hundreds of corner shops as it did so. In consequence continuous efforts were made to reduce production costs, partly by increased efficiency but partly by altering ingredients or using technology to upgrade cheaper ingredients. Like the rest of British industry at the time the food giants favoured low costs and long runs rather than the batch production of quality which was edging in to other parts of the world.

Ironically, when food prices rose in 1973/4, controls came back with the Price Commission, so for different reasons the food industry went through a further period of restricted profits – which also hammered small businesses. Lord Cockfield, chairman of the Price Commission, said in 1978: 'We suffer in this country from market domination, price leadership, parallel pricing, the lack of effective competition, unwillingnesss to compete on price . . . and a cost-plus mentality.' Thus the food industry has been criticised for getting it wrong both in free and in controlled markets – but in both circumstances it has continued to get bigger.

When the Price Commission was swept away in 1979, small shops again suffered. One measure of the success of the supermarkets is that through the 1970s advertising by big food retailers rose by no less than 533% (or one-and-a-half times in real terms) – whereas manufacturers' expenditure fell in real terms by half.

By the mid 1980s, the supermarket's target had changed. Tesco, who had pioneered piling high and selling cheap, had a new chairman who said that no company could get a price advantage for long, that consumers were now willing to pay so quality had moved much higher up the pile, and that better and less highly-processed ingredients were back in favour. Although convenience remained important, it had finally been firmly joined by quality. Together they have dramatically altered many sectors, for example the market for fresh fruit and vegetables.

In the 1950s and 1960s these had been bulk items of variable standards and seasonal availability where growers often made most money with their worst crops – for when supplies were low wholesalers would take everything and anything on offer, while in a glut they would pick and choose and then cut the price as well. Now, produce to be graded, pre-washed and pre-packed is kept in temperature and atmosphere-controlled stores to appear on the shelves all-year-round. To get regular, reliable supplies of fresh foods, supermarkets organise details not just of varieties and growing technologies but even of the precise day of planting. So today vegetables like carrots and tomatoes come from home-grown supplies for ten months in the year and apples like Cox for eight. These changes have seen specialisation and big investment, and, once more, large professional growers have expanded and small ones have given up – and where this has not happened, supermarkets have turned to imports instead.

The march of the multiples is not complete. By 2000 they will again be bigger and fewer as existing trends continue and new ones arise. Electronic shopping and funds transfer, scanning and stock control, will add to the service they offer – and unless things change unexpectedly consumer preferences will support them too.

The latest twist in the food supply chain is catering. Although pie shops had existed for centuries, the arrival of fish and chips began the fast food industry in Britain. In the middle of the last century fried fish sandwiches were hawked around London pubs, but nobody knows when chips replaced the bread and 'Frying Tonight' became a familiar sign in towns everywhere. Then followed a wave of foreign invasions led by the Chinese and the Indians and followed more recently by the Americans. In line with demands for convenience – and reinforced by the initial decision not to charge VAT on take-away food – fast foods have grown faster. They too use the new technologies of prepack and portion control, of cook-chill and microwave. The demand for higher standards of safety and quality control once more favours larger businesses which can afford the investment and have the management skills to standardise dozens or hundreds of shops into rigid drills over all aspects of their business. The fast food chains and franchises will thus continue to rot the supports beneath the traditional British Caff.

CHAPTER THREE:

Food Safety to the Fore

The brief account of food demand and supply since Victorian times shows how tides of surface change overlay a deeper current of continuity. We have been phlegmatic about food. This now shows signs of altering and food poisoning bears a large responsibility for the welcome change in attitude. For until Mrs Currie's notorious pronouncement about eggs we had worried about additives, hormones or pesticides, although these things were minnows to Moby Dick where food health and safety were involved. In a 1987 survey of consumer attitudes, two out of five people said cigarettes were the biggest killers, one in three said it was environmental pollution, one in six that it was ingredients in what we eat, and one in 20 that it was booze that did for us. There was no mention of any risk from food poisoning at all. At much the same time the experts put the relative risks in food like this:

microbial contamination (ie, food poisoning)	100,000
nutritional imbalance (ie, bad diet)	100,000
environmental pollution (eg, heavy metals)	100
pesticide residues	1
food additives	1

In April 1988, the Food Policy Research Unit at Bradford University published a report on food poisoning which said, quite simply, that it was a national disgrace. Author

Dr Verner Wheelock wrote: 'Most people are unaware how bad the current position is today, and, perhaps more importantly, they just do not realise that much of it could be avoided. I believe it is only a matter of time before there is a public outcry about the deplorable hygiene standards that are typical of many food businesses.'

He picked out catering, ignorance and poultry as three areas of threat – and Mrs Currie saw to it that the outcry began just eight months later. Given the assessment that food poisoning is 100,000 times more serious a risk than food additives, the response was astonishingly slow in coming.

There was good and bad in Wheelock's assessment. He attacked kitchens hemmed in by cockroaches and rats, flies and mould. He criticised broiler chickens. He praised the large hotel chains and the food manufacturing industry – though with exceptions. 'It is certainly not my intention to give the impression that the entire food manufacturing industry is implementing everything in the Good Manufacturing Practice (GMP) Guide. There are many small companies as well as some big ones operating on the margins which cut corners and which treat the legislation with contempt as long as they can get away with it. However, the fact remains that those big companies and many of the small companies which, between them, produce most of our food, aim to achieve high standards of hygiene and food safety.' He argued therefore that most food poisoning was in the hands of the catering industry which must clean up its act by applying the controls, expertise and codes of good practice developed by the manufacturers.

Others have issued similar warnings. As long ago as 1981, Daphne Grose of the Consumers' Association wrote: 'In 1972 the number of food poisoning cases notified were about 5,000; in 1979 notifications were over 11,000. The cause is endemic salmonella in herds and flocks combined with bad practice in catering, and on retail, institutional or domestic premises. Some additional powers might help the inspectorate, environmental health officers, to fight the bad practices but this is essentially a question of human behaviour and educating people to behave differently.'

Such education may not be easy. Recently, the *New York Times* produced the following list of foods to avoid serving at meals if you want to keep diet out of the conversation. They were: 'shellfish, nuts, red wine, eggplant, garlic, pork, meat and dairy products, caviar, alcoholic beverages, fats, sweets, fried foods, beef and other red meat, sauces, butter, caffeine, veal, meat in general, any food being boycotted anywhere, rabbit, squid, snails, sweetbreads, venison, offal, snake, bony fish, artichokes, corn on the cob, fried chicken, soups, ribs, poultry with bones, spaghetti or other long pasta, tacos, lobster, starches or breads.' To that any British diner would have to add poultry without bones, eggs, all preserved foods, full fat milk, raw milk, yoghurt and especially hazelnut yoghurt, soft cheeses from Europe, pâté from Belgium – and water from tap and bottle. It won't be long before the only safe thing left to chew on will be the tongue in your cheek – and microbiologists say that has its dangers too.

Microbiologists are a cautious breed. One has recommended keeping soap dry at all times to stop microbes multiplying on it. Another followed the bachelor practice of washing up infrequently – but his wife-to-be found all the dirty dishes kept in the fridge while awaiting the weekly wash. Here is one microbiological account of everyday life in the kitchen.

'A meat stew left open in a warm kitchen for a day or two will collect all the airborne microbes that happen to fall into it, plus those coughed or sneezed about the place by passing humans and pets, those scattered by the wings of insects, those falling off the hair and clothes of the cook.

Imagine that the ingredients have been prepared, put together but not yet cooked, so that, in addition, they are liberally infected with organisms from the cook's hands and have a modest infection of miscellaneous mouth and other contaminants on the cooking vessel, left over from when it was dried up with a contaminated cloth last time it was washed up.

'A depressing prospect, it may sound; but in fact the preparation at this stage is perfectly wholesome. The microbes are mainly dormant, few if any are multiplying and most of them are harmless – though if the cook has a cut finger that is going septic, a few potentially nasty pathogens may be present. Even so, the mixture is harmless because of the small number of microbes present. The meat and vegetable tissue is largely intact, as it was in the living animal or vegetable, the water is pure enough and the salt and flavourings are not much use as nutrients for the microbes. If it were to stand in a warm place for a few hours, the meat and vegetable tissues would begin to break down, partly by the action of the microbes, partly by intrinsic chemical processes, and more nutrient would become available for the microbes to multiply. But for the while the mixture is quite safe.

'Then the cook boils it for some hours, either in a casserole or in a saucepan, and all the microbes are killed. Unless the cook is very unlucky, all the spores are killed too. Assume the cook is preparing a casserole stew: if it were removed from the oven at the end of three hours and served hot, nourishing and, one trusts, delicious food would be provided to which the microbes I wrote about made an undetectably small contribution. Now assume that there is some left over. It has cooled, so that airborne and hair-borne microbes start to fall in it again, and now, because it has been cooked, all the most nutrient juices and substrates have been extracted from the ingredients. The microbes find a perfect, warm culture medium . . .

and they start to multiply.

'Supposing ten staphylococci got into it from someone's thumb as it was carried out at 8 p.m. after dinner. It is covered up, put on one side and forgotten. The kitchen is warm so the staphylococci start to multiply. By 9 p.m. there are 20, by 10 p.m. there are 40, by midnight 160. Now assume that the organisms divide every hour – and in a really warm place they can divide four times as fast as this – then by next day at noon there will be something like 600,000 staphylococci in that stew. It will be beginning to smell a bit, but it will look all right still (the population of microbes has to reach about 100 million in each thimble-full to look bad). However, some rather depressing chemistry will be taking place in it. Amino-acids, components of the meat and vegetable proteins, are being transformed into substances called ptomaines and rather toxic products of the growth of microbes are being formed. Suppose the cook does not notice, but warms it up in the oven for lunch. The microbes will be killed, but the ptomaines will remain, with one of three consequences. Whoever eats it will have an upset tummy, but it will probably be over quite soon. Or they may just find it tastes a bit off but does no further harm. Or they may not notice . . .

'Now just imagine if it had not been a reheated stew, but a pie that had been intended to be eaten cold. Whoever ate it would have ingested a jolly good dose of live bacteria, and if those had happened to be pathogenic, they could have got a nasty infection of the mouth and intestine. This is how most cases of food poisoning happen: pre-cooked food has been stored in a warm place and has not only gone bad faster than it ought to have done, but has grown pathogenic bacteria picked up from someone who handled it during preparation. This is why preservatives are put into prepared foods: they are in fact disinfectants that have a negligible effect on man but keep microbes at bay. Personally, I should often prefer to do without the foods than bear with some of the preservatives that are in common use, but that is a matter of taste.

'Though chemical preservatives are widely used and unavoidable, there are many traditional processes available for preserving food from microbes. Pickling, which is steeping food in acetic acid (vinegar), preserves food by making it too acid for bacteria to grow. Sugaring also preserves, as in jams and syrups, because few bacteria can grow in strong sugar solutions . . . Salting is a method of preserving meats and fish that depends on the fact that most putrefactive bacteria cannot grow in strong brine. If the brine contains potassium nitrate (saltpetre) or sodium nitrate, the microbe called *Micrococcus denitrificans* grows and converts the nitrate into a preservative substance called nitrite. This forms a red compound with meat protein which thus becomes much less susceptible to ordinary microbial attack; such meat is said to be cured. . . It is not really necessary to grow the microbes to cure meat: the chemical sodium nitrite will have a similar effect, but as it is slightly poisonous its use is controlled by law in most countries . . .

'Spoilage of foods by microbes is familiar to everyone. It could be said that the whole distributive and catering trade in civilised communities is based on procedures, traditional or modern as the case may be, designed to delay or arrest microbial deterioration of the product being purveyed. Think of the problems of the distribution of fish, for example, and the manners in which they have been overcome. A whole technology of food microbiology has grown up concerned with the understanding and control of deteriorative, infective and protective processes in the food industry.' That is John Postgate, writing in his book *Microbes and Man.*

The teeming picture he gives gets statistical confirmation from the work of Diane Roberts of the Public Health Laboratory Service (PHLS). She analysed nearly 1,500 outbreaks of food poisoning and came up with the following list to explain them.

contributing factor	number	per cent
preparation too far in advance	844	(57)
storage at ambient temperature	566	(38)
inadequate cooling	468	(30)
inadequate reheating	391	(26)
contaminated processed food	246	(17)
undercooking	223	(15)
contaminated canned food	104	(7)
inadequate thawing	95	(6)
cross contamination	94	(6)
raw food consumed	93	(6)
improper warm holding	77	(5)
infected food handlers	65	(4)
use of leftovers	62	(4)
extra large quantities prepared	48	(3)

These figures show what happens to Postgate's cook in a catering establishment. Nearly all the poisoning comes from letting food stay too warm too long (the reason why there are well over 100% of causes is because more than one cause often contributes to an outbreak of poisoning).

Though by the late 1980s these factors should have been widely known, poisoning went on rising. By 1988 the figure for reported cases had risen to 41,196, with an additional 28,714 cases of gastro-enteritis from campylobacter infections. In 1989 the figures rose considerably again on those for 1988. The Chief Medical Officer, Department of Health (DoH) Sir Donald Acheson, said that 'the increase in foodborne illnesses in England in recent years has been due principally to increases in salmonellosis due to *S. enteritidis PT4* and to camplylobacter. The fact that the increases in food-borne illnesses which have been observed are limited to a few specific types of bacteria gives a basis for the hope that they can be traced to specific causes in the food chain which can be remedied.'

To put the risks in perspective, he said: 'One is about 100 times more likely to die from an accident in the home than from salmonella food poisoning.' He added for purposes of comparison that the 800 reported cases of food poisoning a week in 1988 compared with nearly 12,000 reported weekly cases of sexually transmitted disease.

One year after Wheelock published his report, with his forecast of a public outcry horribly confirmed, he added an update to his earlier work. 'If we are genuinely concerned about the current level of food-poisoning, then it is time that the highest priority is given to cleaning up large sectors of the catering trade.' Poultry, both meat and eggs, needed close attention too. So did educating consumers. As a result of the publicity over eggs, these things have at last begun to happen.

MYSTERIOUS LISTERIOSIS

One of the most puzzling and widespread microbes which contaminates food is *Listeria monocytogenes* (Lm). The recent House of Commons Select Committee on Lm heard evidence from Sir Donald Acheson, who said that 'the organism responsible for listeriosis is widely distributed in the environment and can be found in many samples of soil, water and vegetation. Some exposure to this organism is probably unavoidable and as many as 1 in 20 of the population carry the organism in their gut at some point without harm to health. Lm has the unusual property of being able to multiply slowly at low temperatures including those present in many refrigerators.

'Lm has recently been found in a wide variety of

foodstuffs including cheeses, a variety of cooked and chilled foods and salads. A recent survey carried out by the PHLS found 12 per cent of samples of pre-cooked ready-to-eat poultry and 18 per cent of cooked and chilled meals requiring reheating before consumption, purchased from retail outlets, were contaminated with Lm. Although when the listerial counts were studied quantitatively they were found to be very small, the presence of Lm at any level of concentration in ready-to-eat cooked foods is unsatisfactory as counts can increase during refrigerated storage.'

Acheson made those observations in the course of 1989. Ten years earlier only vets and farmers bothered much about listeriosis. Abortion storms occurred when it infected flocks of sheep and cattle, prevention was uncertain and insurance costly. The illness in humans was infrequent and so far as it was understood at all was thought to come from contact with infected animals.

Then in 1981 there was an outbreak of listeriosis in Canada. Complicated detective work convicted coleslaw. The cabbages cut up to make it had been fertilised with dung from sheep infected with listeriosis, the bug had multiplied when mayonnaise was added to the chopped-up cabbage, and had poisoned some of the people who ate the coleslaw. This was the first clear link between food and the disease in humans. The case of the Vacherin Mont d'Or showed the difficulty of proving this link. Outbreaks of listeriosis in Switzerland occurred from 1983 to 1987 before cheese was shown to be the culprit. As the mould around soft cheese forms – or as the veins spread through blue cheese – so acidity lessens, and this allows any Lm which may be present to multiply. The link between the Swiss outbreaks and infected Vacherin Mont d'Or was finally established by a World Health Organisation (WHO) Working Party in 1988.

We now know that pâté and other meat products, soft

cheeses and some vegetables can be contaminated by Lm, and that the number of cases is rising. There were fewer than 40 identified cases in England and Wales in the mid-1970s, 150 by the mid-1980s, while in 1988 there were 291 cases, including 52 deaths and 11 abortions. Similar increases have shown up in North America and other parts of Europe. It may still be a very infrequent infection but if you get it, it's dangerous.

Horrible though the results of the increase have been the question arises, if this microbe is so widespread, why weren't there more than 291 cases last year? *The Lancet* in January 1989 surveyed the evidence and said: 'All these reports attest to frequent presence of Listeria in a great variety of foods.' But, although we probably eat quite a lot of Lm, it very seldom makes us ill. We are good at resisting it unless our immune systems are affected. In pregnancy, the immune system changes gear; otherwise the growing foetus might be expelled as a foreign body. This makes pregnant women – and pregnant sheep – susceptible, and both the growing foetus and the newborn are at risk as their immune systems are gearing up; so are old people, and patients on drugs to suppress the immune system.

Infections are rising among farm animals as well, where they have been linked to the popularity of big bale silage. This method of sealing grass in large polythene bags gives a less acidic product than clamp silage, which allows Lm to multiply. Dung from infected animals then spreads the microbes widely, although they can also live for long periods on plants, in the soil and in the guts of animals and humans without any need for reinforcement from dung or other discharges.

Lm therefore is widespread, can easily get into food, and when it does can survive over a wide range of temperatures, so can resist both inadequate pasteurisation and poorly refrigerated storage. It is however killed by cooking, and Sir Donald's advice was to make sure reheated food was 'piping hot all the way through'. The popularity of chilled and frozen foods, and the risk of inadequate reheating, between them explain some of the increase in the illness over the last 15 years. Some people, notably Richard Lacey, Professor of Microbiology at Leeds, have argued that if chilled foods contribute, cook-chill foods risk doing so most of all. The initial cooking may not kill all the bacteria and inadequate chilling in storage can allow Lm to multiply. Then if the meal is not served piping hot throughout some bacteria will survive. Lacey worried particularly about microwave ovens both domestically and in hospital and other catering units where poor controls and inadequate reheating could risk outbreaks of listeriosis.

On this question, Sir Donald quoted the PHLS survey referred to above. 'The situation in the survey with respect to food prepared in cook-chill catering units was more reassuring. Only two per cent of the main course items were found to be contaminated with Lm. Seven of the 10 positive items were bought into the cook-chill processing units "ready-cooked", ie they were items of food prepared elsewhere. The strict control laid down would not permit significant multiplication of listeria contaminating such foods once it entered the catering unit, and the items will generally be reheated before consumption.' But, Sir Donald concluded, 'the PHLS study has identified a problem with retail cooked and chilled foods which is being urgently addressed by the Government.'

While the proportion of cases of listeriosis linked to food is unknown, WHO has recently indicated that food is likely to be the primary vehicle of infection – and that 'the total elimination of Lm from all food is impractical and may be impossible.' That leaves a significant risk for pregnant women, where listeriosis has been estimated at one in 7,000 known conceptions. That is why Sir Donald advised pregnant women to avoid soft cheeses – where contamination can be very high and cooking is unlikely – and to reheat cook-chill meals and ready-to-eat poultry very thoroughly.

Dr Barbara Lund, of the Institute for Food Research outside Norwich, says there is no particular link with Lm and cook-chill foods. Instead, she says the link is with extended refrigeration because of the microbe's ability to multiply at temperatures found in fridges. She also says that microwaves, properly used, kill it. In a letter to the *Lancet*, she wrote that temperatures of 70°C were safe for poultry and for pre-cooked chilled food. But 'clearly heating during microwave cooking is uneven, and the presence of relatively cool regions might account for the survival of bacteria when very high temperatures are recorded in other parts of a food.' So she says that recommended cooking and standing times must be observed. 'The use of standing time after cooking is important to allow the heating to be evenly distributed by conduction without overcooking.' Throughout manufacture and catering, she says, good hygiene and temperature control will minimise the risks, and the rules that cook-chill foods must be kept at under 3°C and eaten within five days are safe guidelines for use in hospitals.

Dr Lund's emphasis on the proper use of microwaves was reinforced by a survey of 132 different models carried out towards the end of 1989 by the Ministry of Agriculture (MAFF) and the IFR at Bristol. This found that, when used according to the manufacturers' instructions, 32 left cold spots below 70°C in the food and 12 of below 60°C. The Minister, John Gummer, initially failed in his attempts to persuade the manufacturers to reveal which ovens were not heating food thoroughly but the outcry was such that within the week the electrical manufacturers' association AMDEA had published a list of all makes and models tested showing which were satisfactory. This helped buyers of new ovens but left existing owners uncertain about safety – though manufacturers provided improved cooking instructions to minimise risks and at least one retailer offered refunds to owners of unsatisfactory models. MAFF was criticised by both consumers and manufacturers for the way in which the information was handled but the roundabout outcome was somewhat improved safety when using microwaves.

Before these tests the Association of Community Health Councils looked at cook-chill in hospitals and accepted that if the guidelines were followed then complete destruction of Lm would occur – but there was a serious risk that guidelines would be breached. 'The fear must be that under pressure to keep costs down, cook-chill systems will be introduced on the cheap and that sooner or later a catering disaster will occur.' Better microwaves will lessen the chances of this happening.

Verner Wheelock's report on food safety said: 'Cook-chill is now in use in hospitals throughout the world. It is highly significant that despite the fears currently being expressed, there has never been an outbreak of food poisoning in a hospital, which could be linked to food prepared by the cook-chill method. Since hospital usage is quite extensive, this evidence strongly suggests that the process is safe provided the basic precautions are applied. Without question, this record is very much superior to that achieved with the cook-serve method.'

Certain facts are thus now clear about Lm. It is everywhere; for most of us it is harmless; when it causes listeriosis food is generally the vehicle; susceptible people, especially pregnant women, should avoid high-risk foods, mainly soft cheeses and chilled foods which have not been thoroughly reheated. One source of the increase in listeriosis is changes in food technology including wider use of refrigeration and cook-chill, but this should be controlled by good practice linked to making sure that food is kept cold enough during its quite brief shelf-life and then that it is thoroughly reheated either conventionally or in a properly-functioning microwave.

'Should be', however, remains for the moment something less than an accomplished fact. The House of Commons Select Committee on Listeria urged in January 1990 that shop temperatures for high-risk foods should be 3°C rather than the 5°C required by regulations – and also that manufacturers should come clean on faulty microwaves to ensure thorough and safe reheating.

EGGS AND ENTERITIDIS

Political party fund-raising events include almost any gimmicks, but the Tory evening at Ottringham in April 1988 was a straight-forward affair for a few tables of bridge ending with a buffet supper provided by the wives from food they had cooked at home and brought with them. The buffet included chicken liver, venison, pheasant and mackerel pâtés, ice creams and a mousse. The food was laid out at one end of the village hall at the beginning of the evening, while the ice-cream was brought out in a cold and firm condition when supper was announced. Of the 75 guests at the do, 17 went down with food poisoning. From 14 of the sufferers, *Salmonella enteritidis* phage type 4 (Se) was isolated. The same organism was found at the farm which supplied the eggs to make the ice-cream, and partly-formed eggs recovered from dead birds were also shown to be contaminated. Thus Se from infected eggs was blamed for causing the poisoning.

Richard North, a consultant to the poultry industry in environmental health and safety, has written a detailed study of the risk of food poisoning from eggs and egg products. Of the Ottringham affair he wrote: 'These results became pivotal . . . the outbreak was the only one where ovarian infection (infection inside the egg when it is laid) had been found in a laying flock associated with a food poisoning incident. It was used as the basis for arguing that such infection was the mechanism responsible for the increase in food poisoning associated with eggs.' He claimed that the evidence against eggs at Ottringham was shaky; that chicken liver pâté was as likely a cause of infection; and that if ice-cream was the cause, it had probably been contaminated by something other than infected eggs.

Chickens, like all animals, carry a heavy load of bacteria in their guts and, worldwide, salmonellas are common among them. When they are slaughtered for meat, the carcase is often contaminated by salmonella from this source, which are killed when the birds are cooked. Transovarian infection is much more uncommon. It can and does happen, but there are more obvious ways for egg-based dishes to be contaminated. Salmonellas from droppings which stick to the shell can get into the egg if it is cracked, or washed – which is why washing eggs before sale is against the law. It can get in when the egg is broken before use. It can be transferred directly to other foods by someone who has already touched the shell. Or of course it can come from some totally different source, including food handlers, pests such as flies, the surfaces or utensils used to prepare food, or other food being prepared at the same time.

Over the years, different strains of salmonella have infected chickens. MAFF vet Gwyn Ashton has said that 'occasionally a salmonella develops a particular affinity for poultry and will persist and establish itself in the national poultry flock and become a potential threat to both poultry and human health. *Salmonella thompson* in the 1940s, *Salmonella menston* in the 1960s, *Salmonella virchow* and *Salmonella hadar* in the 1970s all caused disease in poultry and serious outbreaks of food poisoning in humans.' What seems to happen is that the strain in question gets through the gut wall into the internal organs, including blood, but without necessarily killing the birds as a result. It then contaminates carcases directly, and can also enter eggs via the ovaries. The suggestion that *Salmonella enteritidis* (Se) could be a new example first came in the report of the DoH Working Group on Salmonella in June 1988.

There had been very few reports of Salmonella being found inside eggs, though the Americans and some European countries have recently claimed to experience it. Acceptance that this was the cause of the problem was not universal but later that year Richard Lacey was quoted by the *Sunday Times* as supporting such a route of infection. North claims: 'The scientists on the Working Group, as well as Professor Lacey, seemed to have ruled out completely any other means by which the eggs, or egg products, could have become contaminated.' North continued to disagree.

Decisions on matters of food hygiene and safety are split between the DoH and MAFF. As it happened, while the eggs' crisis was developing, the DoH was also coping with a crisis in hospital catering. Contamination, and poisoning, in hospital kitchens was widespread – we have seen it was already caught up in the debate about cook-chill. It now also got caught up in eggs, because of the claim that infection in two hospitals had been caused by raw eggs. A series of meetings betwen DoH, MAFF and representatives of the egg industry took place from June to November 1988 to discuss these issues.

On August 26, without consulting the other parties involved, the DoH issued a public warning on eggs in a press release. On November 18, another in the series of MAFF/DoH/egg industry meetings issued a press release which increased confusion by taking a different line and concluding: 'For the housewife, it is clearly always safest to cook any food thoroughly and eggs are no exception to this general rule, but the risk of any individual egg being infected is likely to be very small'.

On December 3 Mrs Currie said in a prepared statement to ITN: 'We do warn people now that most of the egg production of this country, sadly, is now infected with salmonella.' When she refused to enlarge on that remark speculation was pursued by media pundits who put numbers of infected eggs anywhere from one in 200, to one in 2,000, to one in 7,000 and upwards. Some were to say one in 350,000, or one in 2,000,000. The fact that one end of this proffered range differed 10,000 times from the other might have suggested that nobody was quite sure but there was no time to reflect on that as egg sales collapsed. They fell by half for the next two weeks, and by a quarter for the next three months. Six months later domestic egg-eating, as opposed to eggs eaten outside the home, was still down by a quarter. A year later egg sales remained down by around 10%.

On December 16 Mrs Currie resigned. On December 19, Minister of Agriculture John MacGregor announced a package worth £19 million to meet the costs of destroying surplus eggs and culling infected laying birds. Both developments were seen by the media as victories for the farming lobby, and the second was interpreted to mean the destruction of anything from four million to 50 million birds. Critics of the egg industry clearly thought such avicide well-merited but, luckily for the birds, their owners, and consumers, they turned out to be wild over-estimates. Much of the industry did not help itself by denying the truth of any criticisms while blaming others, for example feed suppliers, for their problems.

That was how the egg crisis broke. It was a messy way to put food poisoning where it belonged, at the top of the food safety agenda, but at least it achieved it. Some of the issues raised seem today as far from being solved as they were when Mrs Currie started it. In particular, no one is yet sure why there has been a continuing rise in food poisoning; nor of the reasons for the part played by Se. We are a bit clearer about the reasons for blaming one source, infected eggs; and there have been various consequences for consumers and producers.

The first to have an authoritative go at some of these issues was the House of Commons Select Committee on Agriculture, whose report on *Salmonella in Eggs* was published that March. Although it accepted that almost the entire rise in food poisoning had been due to the rise in infection by Se, it recognised that the evidence linking Se poisoning to eggs was mainly circumstantial – and that it was very difficult to trace the source of infection. WHO has said 'there is no other zoonosis (disease shared between humans and animals) as complex in its epidemiology and control as salmonellosis'. Partly as a result, fewer than one case in five of salmonella is traced to food, and fewer still to eggs. For example, of 13,004 salmonella poisonings in the year to October 1988, just over 1,000 were attributed to dishes with eggs in them. But despite this low hit rate the Committee felt that 'the Government was right, in looking for the source of the present health problem, to make egg production the first focus of its attention'.

It went on to say: 'The risks to individual consumers cannot be quantified exactly, but, given that the likelihood of an egg being infected with salmonella is very small, and the likelihood of the infection not being destroyed by cooking is even smaller, normally healthy people should feel no cause for concern. Those who consume uncooked eggs or uncooked egg dishes should be aware that these carry a slight risk. Care should be taken to cook eggs thoroughly for vulnerable groups.'

How large is 'very small'? The only way to find out with certainty is to test individual eggs, and all witnesses agreed that was a waste of time. The PHLS said in evidence: 'The examination of shell eggs obtained at random from retail shops and other outlets is not a rewarding approach to the estimation of the risk.'

Quite simply, that means we shall never know how many eggs are infected. All we can do is guess. Thus Sir Donald Acheson offered one in 10,000 and one in 100,000 as possible guesses. When Professor Lacey offered one in 7,000, Sir Donald agreed that too was possible. But he pointed out that, because we eat huge numbers of eggs, even a tiny infected proportion could add up to quite a lot of eggs.

The evidence offered the Committee on this point was strikingly contradictory. The PHLS, Sir Donald Acheson and Professor Lacey said transovarian infection was a key factor in the rise in poisonings. The vets considered this a shaky claim and asked: 'Who knows where the increase in cases has come from?' They were backed by scientists from the Agriculture and Food Research Council (AFRC) who said of the risks of transovarian infection that it was 'the very evidence that we do not have,' and by Richard North who also strongly attacked the reliability of the evidence for significant transovarian infection.

In the face of this disagreement the Committee settled for their 'very small', and went on: 'No single theory can acount for all the observed patterns of infection and we are satisfied that a number of interrelated factors are involved.' They added: 'Effective controls are needed at each point in the food chain; and we deprecate the readiness in the media and in vested interest groups to undermine this approach by looking for scapegoats. Battery farmers have blamed free-range farmers; free-range farmers have blamed battery farmers; they have both blamed feed producers, food-handlers, the Government . . . Such recriminations serve no good purpose. Many people – most of them unwittingly – have contributed in some way to the present rise in the figures; and many people can play a role in reducing them.'

The controls which they supported were: better research; better procedures for tracing food poisoning outbreaks to their source; better monitoring and control of infection in flocks; better control of feeding stuffs; better control of catering outlets and the use of pasteurised eggs in all uncooked egg dishes; better hygiene in the home. 'With the full implementation of the above recommendations, public confidence can be restored in the safety and purity of eggs.'

At the time, this seemed a sensible enough conclusion on the basis of contradictory evidence. A year later, however, those contradictions are still unresolved, the rise in Se poisonings has continued and we still don't know what is causing them. The PHLS and Richard Lacey continue to blame transovarian infection, and Richard North continues to disagree.

Meanwhile, whatever the precise responsibility of eggs, the Government has introduced a number of Orders which tighten up the rules for chicken farmers. Under these Orders the authorities can now take much tougher action against infected flocks – and owners are required to test their own flocks for infection. Tougher controls have also been put in place against contaminated feedstuffs. As well, five voluntary Codes of Practice have been brought in to help control salmonella in commercial laying flocks.

The results for human Se poisoning are uncertain. WHO has said that no technically sound method is certain to eliminate salmonella from laying houses. Even after slaughter and disinfection, flocks in the same building could be reinfected from the environment. But it says that focus on feeds, breeding flocks and overall hygiene and monitoring in commercial flocks does reduce the threat very substantially. Asked whether destroying all egg-producing stock and starting again would work, Professor Bourne of the AFRC told the Select Committee: 'Well, Sweden has gone down this track, as you probably know.

They have a very small poultry industry. They found it to be not only not cost-effective but also ineffective.' In fact precautions introduced by the Swedes have sharply reduced, though not eliminated, salmonella – and Richard North has pointed out that although no Se has been found in Swedish laying flocks, the rise in human Se poisoning in Sweden almost exactly parallels that in the UK.

Similar difficulties confront controls on feedstuffs which, while clearly helpful, are also uncertain in their effectiveness – largely because feedstuffs are very seldom contaminated with Se. The Select Committee again: 'Some people have been quick to blame contaminated feed for the current problem with salmonella in eggs; but we concur with MAFF that, on the available evidence, the role of feed in the transmission of Se should not be exaggerated . . . We consider, nevertheless, that the underlying problem of salmonella in feed needs to be tackled: and the absence of Se is no reason for complacency.'

We are left to face the fact that there is a worldwide problem of salmonella infection of humans and nobody knows quite why or what to do about it – except introduce tighter controls at all levels of the food chain.

Two things however are particularly galling in this country. The first is secrecy. Richard North is especially fierce on this, and has written: 'Another central issue is the way information is being handled. Technical data is contained, protected and handled by a limited number of people who shroud their data in confidentiality worthy of the Official Secrets Act, totally contrary to all notions of freedom of dissemination of scientific and academic information . . .

'With almost sole access to the source material, officials used the information to portray a message of their choice. There has been no ready means of checking the accuracy of their information. Such scrutiny as has been possible indicates that the interpretations of the data are suspect.

'The result has been unnecessary damage to a valuable British industry and wholly unwarranted alarm . . . The key lesson, and recommendation, is that an element of "glasnost" is needed for the health "industry". We seem to know more about the workings of the Kremlin than we do about our own Public Health Laboratory Service.'

The second is our research effort. We have world-class scientific resources which could be invaluable in helping to sort out the facts about salmonella poisoning – and the cash to support them has been cut so that excellent work on salmonella has been abandoned.

So far, therefore, the results of the eggs' crisis have been to alert consumers to risks, to find out that there is no certainty at all that eggs have been solely responsible, and to confuse this both by secrecy and by reluctance to commit resources to tracking down the real dangers. A small number of eggs from a small number of flocks has been infected, nearly a million birds have been slaughtered, and production costs have gone up by over 10%. The price of eggs has risen sharply as a result of shortages, and this has seen a large increase in imports. Many of them come from Holland, where warnings about salmonella in both eggs and poultry meat have recently been given. Some consignments of imported eggs have been found to be contaminated.

Small egg producers have suffered badly from the crisis, leaving the giants to consolidate their position – and some now argue that most domestic independent and free range producers will disappear in the face of higher domestic costs of production and cheap imports.

In a television interview in October, over ten months after the crisis broke, Mrs Currie said she had been wrong. She should not have said 'most eggs'; she should have said 'many' or 'some' or 'a few'. She had found, like the Select Committee, that nobody knows the precise answers. Almost a year to the day after she had made her remark, the House of Commons Select Committee reconvened.

It heard that cases of food poisoning continued to rise sharply but that eggs were no longer the main cause of the increase. Three statistics were offered by the DoH: food poisoning was up overall by 42% in the first nine months of the year; Se poisonings were up 9.8%; of all salmonella poisonings which could be firmly attributed to food, eggs were blamed in 35 per cent of cases compared with 39% in 1988.

Chief vet Keith Meldrum said he felt the measures taken were working, but accepted that with hindsight they had been excessive. Dr Eileen Rubery of the DoH was more cautious. She said there were 'some grounds to hope that the advice we have been giving may have helped in some way.' Given the continuing uncertainties, her claim seemed suitably modest.

WHO SAYS IT'S CATERING?

Food poisoning has increased all over Europe. In 1980 WHO's regional office for Europe started to monitor the rise. In 1981, eight countries joined in; 25 had signed up by 1989. The Berlin-based director of the programme Dr Klaus Gerigk says of the UK experience: 'The same trend was observed in the Federal Republic of Germany . . . For Sweden, as another example, the same holds true . . . Poland and Spain also report a permanent increase of food-borne disease during the last years . . .

'Sweden and the Federal Republic of Germany report Salmonella as the main causative agent with a consider-able share of other microorganisms. In Poland and Spain, cases and outbreaks were mainly caused by Salmonella while in outbreaks reported from France besides Salmonella, *Clostridium perfringens*and *Staphylococcus aureus* played a certain role. Quite often the causative agent could not be identified.

'It is mainly food of animal origin or food which contained parts of it which was involved in foodborne disease outbreaks. Poultry (Scotland), foods containing eggs (Spain), meat, poultry and eggs and egg products (France) and meat and meat products (Yugoslavia) were the food items which played a major role.

'It is evident that mass catering establishments are important places, where food can become contaminated and foodborne disease outbreaks may occur. These establishments include restaurants, hotels, canteens, hospitals and similar facilities, where large numbers of people consume the same food at the same time. But it should also be mentioned that in some countries single cases and household outbreaks seem to have a major share in foodborne diseases (Federal Republic of Germany and Austria).

'The analysis carried out by Diane Roberts on 1479 outbreaks which occurred in England and Wales from 1970 to 1982 shows that in most incidents time-temperature mistakes could be identified, such as too long holding times at ambient temperature, inadequate cooling, inadequate reheating etc. The information given by France and Spain indicates the same features. But it can also be seen from their figures that cross-contamination either by personnel or equipment plays a role . . .'

The Richmond Committee's recent report on the *Microbiological Safety of Food* said: 'Statistics we have seen suggest that up to two-thirds of outbreaks of food-borne illness arise from catering . . . When best estimates suggest that catering accounts for only about 14 per cent of UK food consumption, this seems disproportionate . . .'

All over Europe therefore the same thing has been

happening. All over Europe much the same explanations have been given as Daphne Grose proposed in 1981, Verner Wheelock in April 1988 and both Gerigk and Richmond confirm above. Only in England were eggs put up against the wall and shot. Why?

The House of Commons Select Committee offered this comment. 'Since this Report is founded on the evidence we received, we must put on record that we received many letters from members of the public who viewed Mrs Currie's conduct more favourably than we have done. Sections of the press, too, have championed her as someone who "spoke out" against vested interests. We are not altogether out of sympathy with this body of opinion. Of course the public is entitled to know about health risks in food. Of course the Government must act to reduce the risks. And, of course, anyone who heightens public awareness or stimulates firmer Government action deserves a measure of credit. Pockets of complacency have been punctured: that is all to the good. But we do ask people to reflect whether the public interest has been served by the exaggerated "food scares" of the last two months. Risks are intrinsic to human life. People take a succession of tiny risks every day: there are risks in smoking a cigarette, driving a car, making love, drinking alcohol, walking under a ladder. But a responsible politician should not exaggerate the significance of one risk relative to other risks. Exaggerated public anxiety is itself a health risk; and it often leads to resources being deflected from problems that need them more to ones that need them less.'

Since then, Dr Tom Crossett, chief scientist at the Ministry of Agriculture at the time of the scare, has been quoted in the *Independent* as saying: 'I think the egg was a route of infection, but that it will turn out to be something of a scientific curiosity. As we learned more and more about the situation, the proportion of eggs we could say was infected grew smaller and smaller.'

That leaves a number of complacencies still much in need of the lance. Some of them were vigorously attacked when Dame Barbara Clayton reported on a poisoning which had nothing to do with food.

At half past four in the afternoon of July 6, 1988, a lorry delivered 20 tonnes of aluminium sulphate to the Lowermoor Water Treatment Works. Aluminium sulphate is routinely added to water supplies in small amounts as part of the purification treatment, but on this occasion the chemical was mistakenly discharged not into its normal storage container but direct into the treated water reservoir. From there it gravitated to Camelford, Michaelstow, Tintagel, Boscastle and St Endellion, among other spots, arriving in time to fill kettles, boiled for a late afternoon cuppa, with a weak solution of sulphuric acid. The resulting liquid curdled milk in tea and coffee, formed a blue-green scum with soap which led to severe staining of baths and basins, and discoloured finger nails and hair. Drinking it caused physical symptoms which included nausea, vomiting, diarrhoea, headaches, fatigue, itching skin, rashes, sore eyes and mouth ulcers.

According to Professor Clayton, officials of South West Water assured people that the water was safe to drink. Not only was this bad advice: no authoritative advice at all was available until after press reports of the incident had been published, nor was any full account of what had happened made until weeks later. The response of the authorities was inadequate and unacceptable.

By eleven o'clock that evening, staff at the Works began to flush the mains water into rivers where it killed a very large number of fish, but it was not until July 11 that the water supply was more or less back to acceptable limits, and at least a month before it was fully back within the limits set by the EC Drinking Water Directive. Thus people were exposed to the effects of this accident over several weeks, and for several days received water which was unhealthy.

The major pollutants were, obviously, aluminium and sulphate. These made the water so acid that copper, zinc and lead – normally present in minute amounts from domestic plumbing systems – also rose in concentration. Professor Clayton examined the consequences in her report.

She said the sulphate, copper, lead and zinc would have caused no long-term effects in the amounts analysed, but the rise in copper and in sulphate could have led to tummy upsets while they lasted. Aluminium was a more difficult problem. It is common throughout the environment and occurs in the food we eat, and can get into food cooked in aluminium pots. It may be swallowed directly in large amounts by people using antacid tablets. The chemistry of its absorption is complicated, but the possible link with Alzheimer's disease is thought to relate to constant exposure over decades. Overall, said Professor Clayton, whatever the unpleasantness of the short-term consequences, any long-term effects were most unlikely either from the chemicals taken separately or, as was in fact the case, from the mixture in which they came out of the tap.

Nevertheless, many people caught in the accident complained about their health both at the time and later. The Clayton report does not question this. But, apart from the short-term illnesses, it says it is most unlikely these health problems were caused by chemical-induced toxicity. Instead, Clayton says they were caused by fear.

'We were particularly surprised to find that consumers had been advised that the water was safe to drink despite the unpleasant taste and appearance. In our opinion this engendered much anger and distrust, which was still evident when we visited Camelford in February 1989. Much of the continuing anxiety is attributable to reports in newspapers, radio and television, which have given prominence to alarming statements by some scientists, concerning long-term effects, for which there is no adequate scientific foundation.'

More categorically, 'in our view it is not possible to attribute the very real current health complaints to the toxic effects of the incident, except insofar as they are the consequence of the sustained anxiety naturally felt by many people'.

These complaints included joint and other pains and arthritis, memory loss, poor concentration, speech problems, depression and behavioural problems in children, hypersensitivity, rashes and mouth disorders, and tummy upsets. Clayton reported: 'General practitioners commented that from September onwards each new media report of the possibility of long-term effects was followed by further patients complaining of symptoms which the patients thought were due to the incident. However, the total number of attendances by patients at local practices between May 1988 and April 1989 showed no overall increase. We were particularly struck by reports from patients and general practitioners alike of widespread anxiety throughout the community about the possibility of long-term effects'.

Finally, she added 'the supply of foul tasting, discoloured water, the acute effects on health which followed its consumption, the conflicting advice given about the safety of the water at the time, and statements in the media that serious long-term effects would result, all led to considerable anxiety amongst many local people and to fears for their future health . . . It is common experience that anxiety can itself cause physical symptoms and increase awareness of symptoms due to some other cause. Symptoms due to anxiety are as real and as unpleasant as many of those due to some toxic effect . . . We consider that such further checks as are possible to exclude toxic effects should be completed but that anxiety experienced in the circumstances of the Lowermoor incident is sufficient to explain most, if not all, of the chronic effects which have been reported.'

Further checks have subsequently been done, and at least two arguments made which dispute Professor Clayton's diagnosis. One is that far more aluminium was absorbed by victims of the incident than was previously thought and that the symptoms would indeed be genuine and persistent; the other is that the link to Alzheimer's disease may not depend just on long term exposure to aluminium.

These issues are unlikely to be resolved without litigation. But if the official report is only part right it suggests a complicating condition new to modern medicine, the Clayton syndrome – where complaints of ill-health arise from anxiety caused by official incompetence compounded by scientific uncertainty and media overkill. Such a syndrome offers obvious parallels with several food scares and particularly with the eggs' crisis.

The Clayton antidote is simple. 'Following a chemical accident, such as occurred at Lowermoor, the population and the media should have proper medical and scientific information advice as promptly as possible.' In practice it may be less easy. A senior microbiologist who contributes a light-hearted column to a professional journal once wrote that so little had happened in the world that day that the men in his train compartment all ignored the front page of their paper and turned happily to studying page three. A well-known tabloid shortly afterwards reported equally light-heartedly that 'Scientific Research Proves Page Three is Good For You'.

CHAPTER FOUR:

Hormone Safety and Hormone Black Markets

Ray Heitzman looked at his watch and told himself to relax. One of the advantages of living at Compton on the Berkshire Downs was that he was within an hour of Heathrow. Even so, he wished his partner would stop fiddling about and hit the ball. When he did, it finished up in the rough, but Heitzman had played the eighteenth so often he knew that, with any luck, he would have a playable lie. He was right. Relax, he told himself again. But he rushed it and the shot came out thin to run on over the dry grass and finish in a greenside bunker. His partner's recovery gave Heitzman a thirty foot putt to halve the match. He left it three feet short.

He had time neither for a shower nor for a quick drink with the others in his match. Instead, he drove past the office to collect what he would need in Brussels before heading for the motorway. On his desk his secretary had left the transcript of a cable. 'FOLLOWING THE OPINION RECENTLY GIVEN BY THE EUROPEAN PARLIAMENT CONCERNING THE COMMISSION'S PROPOSAL ON THE USE OF HORMONES THE COMMISSION IS IN THE PROCESS OF CONSIDERING ITS POSITION IN VIEW OF THIS SITUATION I REGRET TO INFORM YOU THAT THE MEETING FORESEEN FOR THE 30TH OCTOBER 1985 IS SUSPENDED UNTIL A

LATER DATE FOLLOWING THE DEFINITIVE DECISION OF THE COMMISSION.

It was signed M BARTHELEMEY, DIRECTOR.

When not playing golf, Dr Heitzman is a specialist on the use of hormones in fattening animals, and a world expert on detecting residues of hormones in livestock carcases. He was a member of the Lamming Committee set up by the European Commission in Brussels to advise on the safety or otherwise of using hormones to fatten livestock.

The meeting planned for October 30th and cancelled so brusquely by Barthelemey, was to conclude five years work on these questions by offering the Commission the advice it had asked for. The other 22 scientists preparing to travel from other parts of the Community got the same cable, but there never was a later date fixed for the meeting. Their work was locked into a bottom drawer and the key was thrown away. Lamming, Professor of Animal Physiology at Nottingham University, was discreet, diplomatic – and furious. Not only had five years' work been binned; the whole principle of scientific advice on what was at bottom a scientific question had been junked. Instead, the understandable confusions and fears of consumers had blown Political fuses in the European parliament, which had voted to ban all use of hormones for fattening livestock.

The results included a hefty nudge towards a trans-Atlantic trade war; a boost to black market use of hormone cocktails, safe, not-so-safe and downright dangerous; and almost as a side-effect less beef, less lean beef and more expensive beef. The origins of this tangled story go back to the late 1970s.

It has recently been told by Michael Leathes and Martin Terry in their book *The Hormone Scandal* (which has not, so far, been published in the UK). Leathes, ex-Secretary General of FEDESA, the European trade federation representing the veterinary products industry, is now based in London and practising the law for which he is qualified in Europe and the United States. Terry, then a toxicologist employed by a veterinary pharmaceutical firm, is back in his native Texas working as a consultant in toxicology and regulatory affairs. Both therefore worked for industry in this dispute but, writing in their joint capacity as lawyer and scientist, they aim to give the public the information needed to decide whether meat in shops is safe. What follows is based on their startling account.

The scandal started in Italy when school children, both boys and girls, were found with enlarged breasts and other alarmingly epicene characteristics. Although all growth promoting hormones had been banned in Italian live-stock production since 1961 a vigorous black market supplied producers with illegal hormones. These were immediately suspect. As an article in the Lancet of August 11, 1979, said 'we could not find a source of oestrogen contamination, but we suspect that an uncontrolled supply of poultry or, more likely veal, may have been responsible.'

Shortly afterwards diethylstilboestrol (DES) was found in jars of baby food. DES is an oestrogen (feminising) hormone which is genotoxic (harmful to the body's genes) and carcinogenic when swallowed in high enough doses. Whether the amounts in the jars were in fact large enough to harm infants, whether any were actually harmed, whether the DES came from cattle or another source, the link was made. Meat was to blame.

Meat markets collapsed. The press called for tougher penalties and stricter controls – and on September 22 1980 an Italian judge banned the sale of all veal, home-grown or imported, throughout the country. Shortly afterwards the Council of Ministers in Brussels also banned DES along with other growth promoting substances, but permitted continued use of five hormones in countries where they were already allowed. These were the three natural hormones oestradiol, progesterone and testosterone, and two others, zeranol and trenbolone. The Commission in Brussels then asked Professor Lamming to chair a committee on the safety or otherwise of these five hormones.

Leathes and Terry confront a number of questions in their book. The first is, why use hormones? In brief, they say, because feed conversion is more efficient, weight gain is faster and the meat produced is leaner. 'Cattle themselves produce certain endogenous sex hormones and farmers top up the blood levels of any hormones that are deficient, by administering additional hormones as implants.' Heifers are given male hormones, bulls female ones and steers get both. The amounts involved are tiny.

For example, steers naturally contain hormones in their tissues which are measurable in parts per trillion (ppt: to find one ppt is about the same as finding a single tennis ball in Wales) and for oestradiol are normally from 1 to 9 ppt. When implanted with additional oestradiol, this may rise from 2 to 13 ppt. Oestradiol in untreated heifers is around 14 ppt and in pregnant heifers or cows is often over 50 ppt. Testosterone in untreated heifers averages 20 ppt; implanting with testosterone raises this to levels from 30 to 100 ppt. In untreated pregnant heifers it is 420 ppt, and in untreated bulls it is 535 ppt, although in many individual animals it may be over 1,000 ppt.

Meat is not the only source of dietary exposure to hormones. A glass of milk contains ten times the oestrogen found in half a pound of steak from an implanted steer. A spoonful of wheatgerm contains nearly 30 times as much, three ounces of peas over 50 times as much, a pint of beer around 300 times as much, and a spoonful of soya contains 2,800 times the oestrogenic activity of the same steak.

The reason none of these foods has any effect on us

when we eat them is that we already make much larger amounts of these hormones in our own bodies. A man produces around 30,000 times more oestradiol every day than the amount in the same steak. A woman produces between 60,000 and 600,000 times the amount, unless she is pregnant when her daily oestradiol production becomes several million times the amount in the average implanted steak. Even pre-pubertal boys, who make less oestradiol than any other human group, on average produce 2000 times the amount in half a pound of steak. In all of us, these levels fluctuate. 'A momentary glance at a good-looking person of the opposite sex, walking along the street, could have far more influence on a person's hormone levels than all the milk, beer, soya bean oil and cabbage they are likely to consume in a week, let alone any beef from hormone-implanted cattle.'

Even so, are hormones safe when used as growth promoters? There is no question they can cause sexual abnormalities in humans – but only if the dose is high enough and long enough. Could that occur from use in animal production? The authors survey the evidence, especially the medical evidence, and write: 'At the end of the day, contrary to cherished popular belief, we are left with the realisation that in the medical literature there is not a single confirmed case of any human sexual abnormality associated with the consumption of meat from cattle treated with hormones. This statement holds true even for the grossest misuse of hormones in animal production – including dangerous hormones like DES. This is not to condone misuse of hormones, not to underestimate their dangers. Nor does it imply that large doses of hormones in food could not cause sexual abnormalities. It is simply an historical fact. And in view of the billions of doses of hormones that have been used in animal production over the past 35 years, that fact requires some explanation.'

The first reason is that the residue of any administered hormone circulating in the tissues is present in very small amounts. 'Unless the consumer eats a steak which happens to contain an illicit injection site with a hidden deposit of unabsorbed hormone, the dose of hormone residue eaten by the consumer will be an infinitesimal fraction of the dose originally received by the animal. It turns out that the consumer dose is about one million to ten million times less than the cattle dose.'

But very small quantities of chemicals can cause cancer. What is the risk of that happening? For more than half a century it has been known that high doses of sex hormones over prolonged periods caused tumours in laboratory animals. In the 1960s there was an increase in cancer in the daughters of women treated with high doses of DES during pregnancy. The Food and Drugs Administration (FDA) in America banned DES from use as a growth promoter in cattle on the evidence of harm of this sort when used in human medicine (or when swallowing vitamin capsules accidentally contaminated with DES, or from harmful occupational exposure during DES manufacture). Because the ban was for those reasons no one bothered then or since to find out whether DES at the levels found in implanted livestock is harmful or not. It may be, it may not be. We don't know. Without actual evidence of safety, the conclusion must be that it is unsafe.

The FDA did however look closely at the risk from other growth-promoting hormones. In 1983 it concluded that the endogenous (natural) sex hormones did not initiate cancers though they could promote them, but that such promotion was dependent on high doses. According to our two authors, 'doses of hormones that are insufficient to cause hormonal effects will also be insufficient to promote cancer' – a version of the Paracelsus doctrine given earlier by James Lovelock. When Lamming's Committee reviewed the evidence it concluded that the natural hormones were safe to use as implants. Indeed, it said that no question of safety arose at all in animals where these hormones had been properly used in an appropriate form. Then it moved on to the more difficult case of the two other hormones. Some of the evidence needed was not available, and Lamming asked for more time to decide the issue. We have seen that, just as his committee was ready to report its findings, M. Barthelemey fired off his cable. Lamming had to wait until October 1987 before a summary of his findings which said that all five were safe appeared in the *Veterinary Record* – but by then it was too late to warn of the dangers of the spreading black market resulting from the ban on all hormones.

The FDA reached the conclusion that properly controlled use of the natural hormones was safe. So did the joint expert committee (JECFA) of the Food and Agriculture Organisation (FAO) and the World Health Organisation (WHO). These groups said the same thing about the two synthetic hormones zeranol and trenbolone.

Leathes and Terry add that 'the carcinogenicity of DES – and specifically the question of whether it is an initiator or promoter of cancer – is still the subject of scientific controversy. As for the other five hormones, however, regulatory scientists the world over have reached a unanimous conclusion – when used as implants in accordance with good animal husbandry practices, they do not cause or promote cancer.'

What guarantee is there that they will be properly used? There can be none. But what is true is that the banned hormone implants are by far the safest formulation for administering growth promoters. Implanted animals absorb the active hormone very slowly – so concentrations are at the parts per trillion levels – whereas illegal injections or the equally illegal sprinkling of hormones directly onto feed lead to very rapid absorption and produce high levels in tissues for a short time after administration. Further, implants are placed under the skin of the ear which is discarded at slaughter. There is no temptation to implant into muscle since that works less well; and the implant dose is fixed at a legally authorised level. By contrast, injections can overdose through accident or ignorance and can result in effective consumer doses millions of times larger than the maximum possible exposure from the use of hormone implants. Thus, though there can be no absolute guarantee of safety, legal implants are certain to be much safer than injections, whether legal or otherwise.

We know that black markets use illegal growth promoting substances and dangerous routes of administration; we know that black markets flourish most vigorously in those European countries where hormones were previously banned; we know that where they were allowed, implants were used. None of that guarantees that legalisation of hormones would ensure only their safe and proper use, but it makes it hugely more likely than under present conditions where dangerous black markets continue to grow.

Why should hormone use be allowed with livestock when it is forbidden for athletes? Often they are the same substances, and further 'the total active dose administered to an athlete or a steer is likely to be in the same range: 20 to 200 milligrams. But there is an enormous difference between athletes and cattle in the rate at which those doses are absorbed. An athlete who takes hormones orally as tablets or capsules absorbs each dose in a matter of hours. The same would be true of a consumer who ingests meat containing the site of a recent injection of black market hormones; the athlete's daily exposure is in the milligram (thousandths of a gram) range. The same would be true for the hapless consumer who eats a black market injection site hidden in his steak. Cattle treated with licensed implant formulation, on the other hand, will take several months to absorb the administered dose, and even then absorption is not complete. The result is that the implanted animal's daily exposure is in the microgram (millionths of a gram) range.'

This exposure is then diluted throughout the animal's body; the hormone is also metabolised by the animal; and it is excreted by the animal as well. 'These three factors of dilution, metabolism and excretion drive the levels of hormone in the edible tissue of implanted cattle down into the range of nanograms (billionths of a gram) or parts per trillion per kilogram of meat.

'This means that the consumer who eats a large steak from a hormone-implanted steer every day has a daily exposure to sex hormones which is millions of times less than the daily exposure of the athlete who abuses the same substances intentionally, or of the poor consumer who quite unintentionally consumes most of a cattle dose of illicit injectable hormone.'

There is a popular view that hormones were banned as a result of consumer pressure. Although that was significant, the beef mountain also played a major part. The European Parliament's vote for a ban on hormones was stimulated by consumer groups but it also presented the Commission in Brussels with what it thought was the answer to the beef mountain. Farmers denied the use of hormones would be hard-pressed to make money from beef, would have to turn to something else, and beef output would fall.

But if consumers and politicians were closely involved, the manufacturers of the hormones also contributed to their own downfall. Those who made and sold the three natural hormones wrestled for advantage against those who who made the two synthetic ones, which not only added to the confusion but stopped any of them from explaining clearly what the benefits and risks of hormones were. They reunited once the total ban arrived – but by then it was too late.

Long before Brussels pulled the plug on the Lamming Committee, a vigorous black market in Europe supplied dozens of bucket-shop hormones. In Belgium the beasts were known from their hugely accelerated growth as turbos. One young Belgian housewife, asked by a BBC Television reporter how she liked these turbo-charged steaks, raised her eyebrows and shrugged. Her family demanded beef; that was the beef her butcher sold. It seemed likely that the ban might see similar reactions elsewhere in the Community.

It did. Now, the black market flourishes mightily. According to our authors, the Mafia are in there and so are the IRA. It will not go away of itself and it is impossible to control. There is too much money in it for all concerned, there are too many interests. There are well over a hundred growth promoting substances, so that detecting them is an almost insuperable problem. While nobody knows whether most of these products are safe or not because the testing has never been done, some of them are definitely known to be dangerous. A number of them are not even formally illegal because until recently nobody considered using them as growth promoters. Finally, there are several million farms in Europe so policing them, especially in close-knit rural communities, is effectively impossible.

An Italian proverb says that the market is stronger than the law, and at present at least half the market for veterinary products there (most of which are said to be hormonal growth promoters) is illicit. It has spread its tentacles into West Germany, Belgium and the Netherlands. In parts of Europe perhaps as many as nine animals in ten are illegally treated. Ethinyloestradiol and other synthetic hormones were found in the meat used for one beefburger in four by the Belgian consumer testing magazine *Test-*

Achats reporting in its January 1989 issue. 'A 50 mg-dose of ethinyloestradiol – an amount which could easily be injected into a veal calf – is the equivalent of about 1000 birth control pills, and just as active when consumed by the mouth.' Now the East Europeans, hungry for hard currency, are joining in the production of growth promoters. Meanwhile the bureaucrats in Brussels have resolutely stood their ground. They have done more: they have vigorously criticised all who disagree with their decision to ban the five hormones, in particular the Americans who continue both to assert that such growth promoters are safe and to use them in their own livestock production.

In retaliation the US has banned Community imports to an equal value to that of its now-excluded beef. As the black market has developed, it has also expressed fears about its servicemen in Europe who eat some 50 million pounds of mostly German beef a year. And the haze of irritabililty provoked by the ban has shadowed negotiators struggling for greater freedom in agricultural trade in the Uruguay Round of the GATT. It is an impressive list of achievements for a ban which is certain to go on doing more harm than good.

BLACK MARKETS AND BUREAUCOCO

In 1988, with the hormone ban firmly in place, the European Parliament appointed a Committee of Enquiry into the Problem of Quality in the Meat Sector – which became for the Committee one of the Problem of Hormones. It was forced to do so because of the burgeoning black market and the risks arising from it that consumers might eat huge amounts of hormones or other substances hidden in injection sites in their beef and veal. From this tricky starting point the Committee moved quickly to an advanced form of rococo bureaucracy. The essence of this novel craft is that, where rococo architecture favoured optical illusion, bureaucoco prefers political or even chemical illusion. The details are set down in an explanatory statement on the committee's findings, drafted by Carlos Pimenta. No connoisseur should be without a copy.

It starts by accepting that the five hormones are safe. Science says so and the Committee 'cannot ignore the conclusions reached by the scientific bodies referred to without sacrificing its credibility as an enquiry committee.' To that sacrifice it then gaily proceeds.

One account of rococo architecture describes its 'meaningless decoration'. The explanatory statement has worked an exquisite example. Having agreed that it must not ignore scientists, the Committee reminds itself however that scientists may be wrong and that society, not scientists, must decide about controversial issues. 'If that decision proves to be incorrect, science is not blamed or used as a scapegoat. If this were not so, then we would risk, at the extreme, rejection of science itself by society which could take civilisation in a retrograde direction.'

The meaningless decoration is that nobody suggests that scientists should take such decisions. Parliaments make laws, and judges and ministers – or bureaucrats – interpret or extend them. Why a committee of enquiry should fear that scientists are usurping those functions it does not make clear. Why it should claim to protect its advisers by rejecting good advice it does not make clear.

It ignores the fact that, when parliaments or bureaucrats take scientific advice which turns out to be wrong, science and bureaucracy are blamed impartially, the one for giving and the other for taking bad advice. It further ignores the reality that society is as hard pushed to reject bureaucracy as to reject science, however much it might like to do either of those things.

The same account of rococo architecture calls it 'excessively ornate'. The Committee obliges. The hormones are safe, but there is a risk that they may be used dangerously – for example, in the wrong part of the animal or too soon before slaughter. Since safe use cannot be enforced, all use must be banned. Why is this excessively ornate? If made a general rule it would see the end of cars, hair dryers, rolling pins, boxes of matches and . . . well, and a lot of other things. There is no mention of our usual course which is to reduce the risk, perhaps by speed limits, perhaps by using safety matches, perhaps by any other straightforward use of common sense.

Then it tries the 'tastelessly florid'. This takes the form of a three-card trick. First card; the consumer need not be logical, may for example reject hormones while smoking and 'will do so of his own free will'. Second card; consumers are confused, and will be stumped by choice if hormones are allowed. Third card, if choice was allowed in this case, then why not legalise everything, including hormones known to be dangerous. The tasteless floridity of this would satisfy the Knave of Hearts.

It has a go at 'freedom from classical restraint', thus. 'The Enquiry Committee is convinced that no amount of control and criminal sanction will ever succeed in totally eradicating the problem of the use of artificial aids to weight-gain and growth in animals.' In short, a ban on the five hormones is not enforceable – not least because of the obvious difficulty, effectively the impossibility, of knowing when natural hormones have been used.

Then it tries 'freedom from utilitarian purpose'. 'A strong economic incentive exists for producers to make their animals gain as much weight as possible, in the shortest possible time. Increased consumer preference for lean meat, low in saturated fats and hence in cholesterol, has given an added incentive to the use of hormonal substances.' Hormones thus help produce cheap, lean

65

meat but nevertheless should be banned.

There is much more of the same, for bureaucoco shares yet another feature with its architectural original: the more shell-work and scroll-work, the more colour and curlicues you add, the more your admirers will applaud your illusion. But alas, where rococo reached heights of richness satisfying to some, bureaucoco is condemned to remain a pastiche.

All these conclusions were reached despite the simultaneous admission that consumers do not and cannot have sufficient confidence in the quality of meat 'as regards the illegal use of hormones and other growth promoters'. But the black market did nothing to discourage the Committee which said that 'the maintenance and reinforcement of the total ban on the use of hormonal and other growth-promoters is the only way to restore (sic) consumer confidence in the meat sector . . .' Thus did it ignore Healey's first law of politics, which states, When in a hole, stop digging. The Committee claimed to have a powerful spade, namely that 'inspection along the entire production and distribution chain of both meat and veterinary medicines should be carried out by multidisciplinary teams of veterinary, public and environmental health, fiscal and police authorities'.

As a supplementary digging tool the Committee wished to encourage, in the meat industry, quality labels similar to the *appellation controlée* in wines, for it felt that voluntary self-monitoring of such quality labels would be the most effective and cheap way of ensuring proper controls and gaining consumer confidence. Had it not heard of, or had it forgotten, the scandals in the wine industry?

It went on to say 'that proven necessity and socio-economic desirability should be criteria of acceptability' despite the severe difficulties of assessing such criteria. But, with a proper regard for theatre, these wise men from Gotham left the best till last. 'With regard to producers castrating male bovines in order to allow open-field pasturage and thus producing animals with lower levels of endogenous hormones than is the case with uncastrated males, the Commission should help fund a marketing campaign for this low hormone-level meat, aimed at consumers concerned about hormone consumption.' You may not put natural hormones in; you may cut their balls off. For some inexplicable reason, the Committee did not recommend hysterectomy and ovariectomy as well, to reduce the dangers of eating hormone-filled beef from what they would no doubt call female bovines.

For good measure they then urged the Commission to go for a world-wide ban on hormones as part of the Uruguay Round of the GATT, a proposal which appeared in part provoked by their eager anticipation of the certain American reaction.

Two things may save consumers from the consequences of this muddle. The first is the law. On December 13, 1989 an oral hearing took place in the European Court in Luxembourg. The action was a representative one brought by the veterinary products industry under the umbrella of FEDESA, the industry's European trade association. It charged that there were no proper grounds for the ban because there are no dangers to animal or human health from using the previously permitted hormones. It was improper to ban products which the relevant expert committee had already accepted as meeting the established criteria of safety, efficacy and quality. The Court's decision will not be available until the early summer of 1990, but if the claims are upheld the ban on the hormones will go.

The second is continuing encouragement of organic farming. Both the Community and individual countries are moving towards a system of standards for organic production backed by controls and identified by labels. That would give people who don't want to eat hormone-implanted meat a choice. Because all meat contains hormones there have always been problems about labels claiming hormone-free products, but a well-authenticated organic label gets round this. Although like the Committee's appellation controlée scheme it is open to abuse, it is far more feasible than policing the black market out of existence.

What the Committee of Enquiry and the European Parliament are trying to support is more extensive farming and an end to surpluses. So they should be. But all the evidence is that they have chosen a rotten route. The consequences of that choice, bad already, will be much worse once the single European market arrives. The House of Lords Select Committee on the European Communities reported on *Health Controls and the Internal Market* in May, 1989. The prospect of the free movement of animals, plants and foodstuffs filled it with alarm. Anyone in the least familiar with the malarkey practised under the Common Agricultural Policy and the criminal conspiracy involved both there and in the hormone black market would find it hard to disagree. As their Lordships put it, 'the only secure time to relax or dismantle frontier checks is when the need for them has been demonstrated to have disappeared. This will not happen until there is a common health regime, yet the Commission proposes to do away with frontier controls before even the legislative framework has been agreed on the alternative means to be adopted to protect animal, plant and human health from contamination by goods imported from other Member States or third countries.

'This is irresponsible. The Commission appears to have sacrificed the practical realities to the ideology of the single market in a mistaken belief that the economic advantages of dismantling frontiers outweigh other considerations.' One of these practical realities would be recognition that controlled use of legally permitted hormones is far safer than a ban and a black market. As things stand, British consumers will be more likely to bite into illegal hormone cocktails in their meat as the Single Market approaches.

ANTIBIOTICS' RESISTANCE

Antibiotics cure sick animals, and prevent disease from breaking out where they are housed in large groups. They are also used to increase growth rates of chickens, pigs and beef animals.

Few, other than say Christian Scientists, would quarrel with the first of these uses, where a ban on antibiotics would lead directly to animal suffering. More would line up with Christian Scientists when it comes to preventive use – though drugs are commonly used for preventive human medicine – even though such a ban would also increase animal suffering, and could see more microbes getting into our food.

Opponents of preventive use are often also opponents of intensive farming. They argue that, if animals were not held in large groups, such drug use would be unnecessary. This is partly true, if only because producers can readily face the loss of 20, but not of 20,000, chickens. If such use ended (unlikely, since it is tough to make a living off 2,000 let alone 20 birds) a chicken dinner would become more expensive and, unless shopping patterns changed over-night, there would also be much higher transport costs.

Some consumers would be happy to meet these costs; others want cheap chicken, so long as they know it is safe. Efficient intensive farmers can use fewer preventive drugs by careful hygiene, like moving animals in and out in batches and disinfecting carefully between each batch, putting sick animals in isolation pens, and getting rid of dung and slurry conscientiously. They can also make sure any drug is withdrawn from use early enough to stop it getting into the food chain. In such ways they can minimise the risks from preventive drug use.

More people still line up against using antibiotics to promote faster growth and thus cheaper meat – even when these are poorly-absorbed, gut-dwelling drugs which do not generally pass from the animal's intestine to the meat, and when, as in this country, they are not used to treat or prevent disease in animals or humans. Nobody quite knows why they work: they are thought to alter the balance of intestinal microbes to help the animal digest nutrients more efficiently. Often, they are fed to poultry and pigs with preventive drugs – and in Sweden a ban on this use has seen diarrhoea in pigs rise by 50%. Thus there is a risk of more suffering from such a ban, as well as more expensive pig and poultry dinners – costs which, again, some people would be happy to meet.

In any of the above uses, there are two possible risks to consumers. One is that antibiotic residues may get into our food where they can cause allergic reactions in some people. The other is that bacteria develop resistance to antibiotics, and will do so faster the more widely they are used. So there are two questions about using them with animals. Are they safe? Do I want to eat food grown like that?

The second depends on your values, which are often kept in your pocket. Remember Brecht who said: grub first, then ethics. Those who have enough grub and have reached the ethical stage (more and more of us) can afford to choose. Others whose pockets are emptier will want cheap food, so long as it's safe.

Joy Wingfield, speaking to the Royal Pharmaceutical Society Conference in September 1989 on the question of safety, said: 'This question has been the subject of widespread debate and shows little sign of ever reaching a definitive conclusion. Linton asserted in 1981 that further restrictions on antibiotics in animal medicine were fairly pointless without greater controls on those used for humans. By 1986, Skovgard concluded that it was unlikely that antibiotic residues in meat actually induced bacteria resistance in the consumer. Conversely, a Californian study into a large outbreak of salmonella in hamburger meat in the same year linked it to subtherapeutic use of penicillins and tetracyclines in animal feed. In Britain, a report by the Steering Group of the State Veterinary Service National Surveillance Scheme published in 1987 found sulphadimidine residues in over half of kidney samples tested.' Unwelcome though this last fact is, the amount swallowed by anyone unfortunate enough to meet the highest concentration found has been calculated at 0.009 grams; this compares with the approved daily human intravenous dose of 7.5 grams.

Further evidence has come from studies carried out by the American government in response to the claim that subtherapeutic use of penicillin and tetracyclines as growth promoters (permitted in the US) might make typhoid fever difficult or impossible to treat.

The evidence assembled rejected this claim. According to the British Veterinary Association (BVA) 'for the first time, a legislative body accepted that low subtherapeutic concentrations of antibiotics in feed do not present a hazard to man because they do not exert selection pressure' leading to resistance. Rather, it is intensive use, in animals or humans, which results in resistance.

Nevertheless, Joy Wingfield points out that risks arise from uncontrolled use. Since this occurs too frequently there is, she emphasises, certainly no cause for complacency. But the BVA is equally clear that 'antibiotics are extremely valuable medicines and that their correct use in animals poses no risk to the consumer'. Although the EEC has controls to stop dangerous animal medicines being used and to monitor food for residues of permitted drugs, these may be poorly enforced. It's the black market problem in a new guise. As Wingfield puts it: 'The colossal bureaucracy devoted to the collation and scrutiny of licence applications is a waste of time if unlicensed medicines are easily available.'

The British tolerate this bureaucracy but, as Mr H Carter of the Royal College of Veterinary Surgeons has put it: 'There is a cultural problem in attitudes to certificates and application of laws and so on in various countries. I do not wish to go any further than that, but everybody knows that that is the case.' He means that a lot of people in Europe can't be bothered with them. As with hormones, there is a vigorous black market in these drugs in much of Europe, which both supplies them more cheaply and avoids paying professionals, mainly vets, to administer them. It almost certainly cannot be policed out of existence but if the professionals could be persuaded to cut prices on these drugs it would be undermined. A subsidy would encourage them to consider this.

Like the BVA, Wingfield argues that the drugs are necessary. 'If profligate and uncaring use of antibiotics leads to a total ban on their use, the implications for human and animal health are disturbing. The animals themselves will suffer considerably from the greatly increased incidence of disease, food of animal origin will become more heavily contaminated with micro-organisms and the economic basis for the production of cheap food through intensive farming would be destroyed.' The black market, which Mrs Wingfield reckons supplies 90% of the Italian demand and perhaps 30% through much of the rest of Europe, would spread – and again many fear that 1992 can only add to the problems in countries where the black market remains small.

There is a further aspect to the risk of resistance. Writing in the *Veterinary Record* in April, 1987, Professor

Richard Lacey gave a personal view of this. He said: 'It is not my intention to claim that veterinary use of antibiotics does not produce problems of resistance – but that if we really do believe that levels of antibiotic resistance in "human" pathogens are unacceptably high, then we must look primarily at human, not veterinary use of antibiotics.' Human misuse of antibiotics is so widespread – for example, over-the-counter sales of chloramphenicol in Central and South America, Africa and Asia, as well as prescription misuse in Europe – it is difficult to see how animal use can make a substantial contribution to resistance in human bacteria.

Although resistant bacteria found in animals can colonise man, anyone who believes that this contribution is substantial must show it to be the case in properly constructed experiments. 'At present, no such data have been published,' said Lacey.

In conclusion, he asserts: 'The whole field of this work has been marred by a lack of objectivity from scientific workers, the media and the regulatory authorities. At present, the veterinary use of antibiotics is essentially irrelevant to problems of resistance to antibiotics in bacteria that cause problems in human medicine.' That does however leave the risks of allergic reactions from residues – and once again, while British farmers are by no means blameless, the Single Market may bring a rise in antibiotic residues in our meat.

CHAPTER FIVE:
Tolerance and Intolerance: Natural and Synthetic

Toxicology – the dose/response relationship to poisons invoked by Paracelsus – may be a shaky science but it has rocklike foundations compared to our knowledge of food intolerance. Dr Jonathan Brostoff, Consultant Physician and Reader in Clinical Immunology at the Middlesex Hospital Medical School, asks in his book *Food Allergy and Intolerance*: 'Why is there so much disagreement over food intolerance? And why do so many doctors regard it as a "media illness", the outcome of ill-informed publicity?' There is, he says, no simple answer.

Brostoff and co-author Linda Gamlin quote the medical historian Dr William Bynum. 'There is a general reluctance among the medical establishment to accept things that are non-specific and don't always cause the same symptoms. It smacks too much of the old ideas of causation in medicine – cold weather was supposed to cause head-colds in some people and rheumatism in other people and so on. Causal thinking before the germ theory was extremely loose and it did not satisfy the usual canons of scientific explanation about cause and effect. There has been a strong reaction to that, and the problem with so-called food intolerance is that it goes against the grain of present-day thinking.'

Symptoms of food intolerance, for example head or gut aches, can be caused in all sorts of different ways. That greatly complicates diagnosis. Worse, though Brostoff says that psychosomatic illness can both cause and be caused by intolerance, orthodox medical opinion is outraged at the idea of foods causing depression, anxiety, hyperactivity or even psychosis. Worse still from the orthodox view, even in well-conducted scientific studies the attitude of the experimenter can apparently influence the outcome: believers are more likely to get positive results, unbelievers to get negative ones.

It is thus hardly surprising that fierce controversy abounds. But Brostoff points out that medicine is not an exact science, and diagnosis of what is wrong with any one of us may be even less so. We differ by nature, nurture, age and sex, all of which can influence health, illness and the way we respond to treatment.

The result is that nobody knows how widespread food intolerance is. 'Estimates of how many people suffer from food intolerance range from a very conservative 0.3 per cent to a rather implausible 90 per cent. Most of the doctors who study food intolerance in the UK would put the figure at somewhere between 10 and 25 per cent.' If that is true, it may be that one in four of us reacts poorly to ordinary everyday foods.

To many people, that seems absurd. Indeed, the authors accept that much of the medical prejudice is based on the idea that food can't possibly be bad for us. But they point out that 'in the wild, most food items are reluctant food items. They do not want to be eaten, and their efforts to stay off the menu are part of what Charles Darwin called the "struggle for existence". Most animals can run away, or fight back, but plants do not have this option.

'Their defence is based partly on thorns and prickles,

but far more important than these is the array of invisible chemical weapons that pervade almost all plant tissues. Some of these simply taste bad, others cause vomiting or other ill-effects. A few even mimic the hormones of insects or mammals and thus disrupt their growth or sexual development.'

Animals adapt to their food as they evolve, and omnivores like certain of the primates, or like rats, have very effective systems for dealing with a wide variety of poisons. As Brostoff and Gamlin comment, 'being an omnivore – an animal who eats adaptably, taking whatever is available – is a high-risk, high-return strategy in the natural world. It opens up a huge range of foods, but makes it impossible for the omnivore to adapt to the specific chemical toxins of a single food source . . . A powerful set of detoxification enzymes is something every good omnivore needs.'

Even so, humans face a unique problem. Most of the foods we eat in large amounts have only been domesticated within the last 10,000 years, which is too short a time for all of us to have adapted despite our natural advantages as omnivores. A comparatively new crop like wheat may lead to trouble in those of us who have an inadequate kit of enzymes to cope with it. According to Brostoff, wheat and milk are more often implicated in food intolerance than any other foods, while rice, maize and soya are also commonly involved – and cereals can cause much more serious illnesses like coeliac disease. Although natural selection long ago removed genes which were fatal in the new environment of agriculture, those causing mild ill-effects would persist for much longer. Minor problems with a new food could easily last for thousands of years.

The medical debate about how far they do so is greatly complicated by the activities of many unqualified practitioners. When the news on food intolerance, and what it might do for those with migraines, irritable bowel syndrome and other long-term illnesses filtered through to the general public despite medical disapproval, people wanted action. 'These patients represent a large segment of the population whose need for treatment is not being met by conventional medicine. Not surprisingly, many people have turned to alternative therapies . . . Many of these therapists have little understanding of nutrition – or of food sensitivity for that matter. Some have endangered the health of their patients.'

The journalist Duncan Campbell in a recent article in the *Sunday Correspondent* wrote of these developments: 'The new pill companies work with an accessory network of magazines and writers, conferences and shows supported directly or indirectly by their advertising . . . The vitamin industry's primary retail outlets – the growing network of High Street "health shops" – sell tubs of pills and the books and magazines which go with them side-by-side with organic vegetables and wholemeal bread.'

Although this market is increasing throughout Europe and America, Campbell says that Maurice Hannsen, president of the European Federation of Health Product Manufacturers, opposes the advent of the Single Market in 1992 because new regulations and the need for scientific tests of safety, quality and efficacy will challenge the trade in 'food supplements'. This would undermine its growth, and could even affect Hannsen's own interests in products like Bio Harmony, which claims to offer the chance of avoiding old age.

Indeed, Campbell quotes Hanssen as claiming that 'age is a preventable illness' – though also conceding that nobody lives forever.

Worries about food intolerance, food supplements and the boom in quackery have led to the formation of the Campaign Against Health Fraud, launched because quackery has crept out of its minority corner and is invading the reputable news media.

Doctors angered by these developments have mounted

a crusade against the whole idea of food intolerance as a commonplace illness, attacking everyone involved from qualified professionals to alternative and fringe practitioners. These attacks have given the whole field a disreputable image and increased the reluctance of most family doctors and consultants to take food intolerance seriously. But, say Brostoff and Gamlin, 'we believe that the scientific evidence is now strong enough to merit a major medical rethink on food intolerance' – and they add a warning about the risks of pursuing any of the fringe practitioners rather than finding a qualified doctor who is interested and can offer help.

These arguments throw light on the equally vigorous controversy about the contribution of food additives to food intolerance – though disagreement here has arisen much less from division among the professionals than from outside critics. They attack additives as both risky and unnecessary. Risk and need are quite distinct and should be kept so, but have often been linked by campaigning critics who know how effectively fear energises media reactions. The Clayton Syndrome rattles its bones in the additives debate.

The Consumers' Association (CA) published a guide to food additives in 1988. It said: 'Over the past 30 years changes in food technology have revolutionised our food supply. Improved delivery, packaging and storage techniques have made it possible to supply a wide range of fresh fruits and vegetables throughout the year. The variety of processed products is as never before, and new methods of processing and preservation have led to the marketing of products as diverse as pot noodles and instant desserts. Whereas at the end of the Second World War, fewer than 1,000 different products could be found in the shops, there are now about 10,000, and they form about three-quarters of the average diet.'

The post food-rationing binge which swung in during

the 1960s offered what one commentator called 'a wonderful world of new products and experiences to an excitement-starved generation who'd never had it so good, and were still unaware of how good they could have it. The marketeer had only to tell them about it and they flocked to the stores who were allowed to stock it. The innovative manufacturer had the world at his feet.' During those years getting on for 8,000 new food products were launched as manufacturers and consumers indulged their new freedoms. Although as we know the large majority failed, innovation has gone on briskly ever since.

As the CA guide put it: 'Changes in food technology have been accompanied by extensive use of food additives to preserve, increase safety, aid processing, and improve the marketability of products. It has been estimated that the use of additives may have increased ten-fold between 1955 and 1985 . . .

'Although over this period legislators gradually extended the controls on substances and drew up lists of about 330 permitted additives which could be legally added to foods, the changes in the use of additives went largely unnoticed by the British public, as manufacturers were not required to state in detail what went into products.

'It is hardly surprising, therefore, that the introduction in 1986 of improved food labelling, which had been intended to provide people with better information about ingredients and additives in processed food, caused a public outcry. People associated the appearance of 'E' numbers, a shorthand code for the additives approved for use in the European Community, with the introduction of new additives whose use they questioned. Misinformation, media coverage of potential safety hazards from some permitted additives, and worries about allergies all added to the confusion and concern.'

Professional concerns about allergy developed in the

mid 1970s, and by 1984 a number of books had emerged which attacked additives and their safety. Before that, some manufacturers and retailers were already taking additives out of their products, but there was little planned industry response until the Food and Drink Federation (FDF) announced a campaign to explain the use of additives in early 1986. It was half-cocked. Major manufacturers and retailers continued to remove additives from their products.

They had been used for a very long time. Salted meat and fish kept our forebears going through centuries of winter. More people have blessed and cursed salt pork than any other food. Salt removes water from the tissue, which dehydrates and kills microbes.

When nitrate is present as an impurity, it turns the meat the pinky-red of bacon and ham. At some point somebody twigged that saltpetre was the best form of nitrate to add colour and taste to meat, and the pickling industry got going. From the start it included sausages, salamis and fancy meats of all kinds, but Hannah Glasse's *Art of Cookery* summed up the no-nonsense approach in 1748. To Pickle Pork: Put a Pound of Saltpetre; and two Pounds of Bay-salt to a Hog.

So we went on for 150 years until we found out that, in the process of curing, the nitrate turned into nitrite, which was in fact the chemical which did the job. So then we gave up adding saltpetre and instead added small amounts of nitrite direct – until 1956 when it was shown that nitrites can form another compound, nitrosamines, which caused cancer in laboratory animals.

Sausage-eating sagged at this bad news; then it was realised that there were other, larger sources of nitrites in the diet, such as vegetables, or even water, and sausage-eaters got stuck in again. Twenty years after that, it was suggested that nitrites might cause cancer directly. This finding has been questioned by later work, but it was enough to start a battle. Meat curers pointed out that some meats, and especially sausages like salamis, were eaten uncooked and that nitrites were essential to kill the bacteria causing botulism – a word derived from the Latin for sausage. Some consumer groups argued that all nitrite did was to make meat a pretty pink, and that meats which were cooked, like bacon, should not be treated, especially since cooking at high temperatures increases nitrosamine formation.

The ground shifted when ascorbic acid (vitamin C) was used in pickling mixtures. It enhances the action of nitrite, so less is needed, and at the same time it slows the formation of nitrosamines, so any risks in using nitrite are reduced. This led the American author Harold McGee to comment that 'orange juice at breakfast and tomato in a BLT may be better for us than we had realised'.

Then interest developed in nisin, a natural antibiotic preservative active against listeria and *Clostridium botulinum*. It is one of the lactic acid bacteria – which sour milk and help cheese resist going off – and appears to work in harness with nitrite to allow even less to be used. Other natural preservatives may come from the family of lactic acid bacteria, although the use of antibiotics in food is discouraged and may well be stopped.

Another shift occurred when it was shown that nitrite does, in fact, help prevent bacterial spoilage and, as the meat curers claimed, specifically acts against the bacteria causing botulism. So, nitrite is now recognised as a food additive which is a preservative, improves flavour and gives the familiar pinky-red colour.

Where does all that leave us in the nitrite war? First, although nitrosamines cause cancer in experimental animals, there is no evidence that eating pickled meats has led to the disease in humans. Second, as McGee has put it, 'thanks to a growing understanding of food chemistry we will be able to continue to enjoy cured meats, once a necessity and now a largely pleasurable choice, with an even smaller exposure to possibly hazardous nitrite.' The hams of our forebears may have contained as much as 50 times more nitrates and nitrites than they do today. Third, those of us who don't or won't eat pickled meats can eat nitrate-rich vegetables safe in the knowledge that they are also eating a lot of ascorbic acid with them. And fourth, deaths from stomach cancer are falling in many countries, and certainly in England and Wales. Nobody knows quite why, but some think it is because of all-round improvements in our diet. Nevertheless, the battles fought over nitrate were to be repeated over other much less venerable additions to our food.

HOW NEGATIVE ARE ADDITIVES?

The CA's *Understanding Additives* says that 'in general, food additives are used for three main purposes:

- to preserve food and prevent the growth of harmful organisms such as bacteria, thereby improving the keeping quality and hence the safety of food. This is their most useful function since bacteria and moulds can produce dangerous and potentially lethal toxins such as those which cause food poisoning
- to modify the consistency and texture of processed products such as soups, desserts, cakes and cooked meats, which affect the way food feels in your mouth
- to add colour and flavour to many foods, from squashes and yoghurts to cheese and pickles. This affects our sensory perception and appreciation.'

The preservatives we use today may be chemical, physical or a mix of both. Chemical methods range from traditional salt, sugar or vinegar to a range of more recent substances some of which are synthetic and others natural. A technology like canning uses a mix, including heat, the physical barrier of the can, and chemicals old and new to preserve the contents.

A significant group of chemical preservatives is the anti-oxidants, used to stop fats going rancid. Ascorbic acid (vitamin C) is an anti-oxidant, as are the tocopherols (vitamin E). Laboratory studies with animals have hinted at possible cancers from using BHT (butylated hydroxytoluene), BHA (butylated hydroxyanisole) and PG (propylgallate); but they have also shown adverse effects when animals are fed rancid fats, which BHT, BHA and PG keep in check. Despite the uncertainties about these studies, substitute preservatives would be welcome and it seems likely that eventually anti-oxidants will come from the natural vitamins and their derivatives. Many food manufacturing companies are already using citric acid and vitamin E rather than BHA/BHT.

Since the uninhibited splurge of the 1960s there has also been a steady move away from chemical towards physical treatments, which include freezing, heating and packaging. Fruit juices are likely to be pasteurised rather than chemicalised – and in milk where this innovation started chemical preservatives are no longer permitted. In fruit yoghurts, better quality control, quicker turn-round times and chilled distribution have replaced preservatives. In crisps and snacks, better oils and quicker turn round times have got rid of anti-oxidants. Faster distribution, better temperature control throughout the food chain, and rapid turnover reduce both shelf life and use of additives. They do however raise costs, especially energy costs, of processed foods.

Flavours, like preservatives, have a long history. For centuries, pepper was the most prized commodity in world trade. It was pepper that the Portuguese brought back from their early voyages to India and the East Indies and pepper that Columbus set sail to find in 1492, thus extending its influence in our affairs all round the world to the west as well as to the east. If pepper was king it had a large court of attendant spices which were widely traded and much used both for flavouring and preserving food.

After the spices, probably the best-known flavouring substance is MSG (monosodium glutamate), beloved of the Chinese but dear to seaweed eaters everywhere; it is closely followed by the sweeteners like aspartame or saccharin. There may in all, however, be 3,000 flavours used in Britain. If that sounds excessive, nature has taken a somewhat similar path. Honey is thought to have over 200 different flavour ingredients, as have many fruits; even such traditional tastes as Scotch whisky can have over 300. Such profusion is one reason why neither here nor in Brussels is there a permitted list of flavours, though there has also been commercial resistance to the suggested restrictions.

When the Food Additives and Contaminants committee looked at flavours as long ago as 1965 it identified a number which should not be allowed in food. It repeated this warning in 1976 but neither the Labour government of the time nor the subsequent Conservative government acted on the recommendation. Now the EEC is struggling with the problem, and will eventually produce a list of permitted natural and artificial flavours. Meanwhile, in the absence of comprehensive labelling, consumers cannot be certain which flavours have been added to what products. Perhaps the least unsatisfactory aspect of this is that we swallow very small amounts of these additives, on one calculation only 1/10,000th of the quantity of artificial preservatives. As with preservatives, synthetic flavours – which can be used to replace nutrients in cheaper products – are giving way to herbs, spices and other natural foods and flavours. Much work is devoted to growing the shoot or root cultures which hold the flavours so they can be harvested more effectively and cheaply.

Adding colours to food has come in for widespread criticism. History is against it for if canning and colours have always been first cousins, confectionery and colours are almost twins. There is an old-established connection between colour and flavour, perhaps linked to a feeling that grey means danger, bright and clear mean fresh and palatable. If so, it led to manipulation by the unscrupulous. Some of the things sold 100 years ago as sweets and confectionery pass belief. Red lead made a pretty contribution to a boiled sweet, as did copper arsenite if green was what you wanted. The arrival of aniline dyes late last century was little more than a retreat from awfulness, but in Britain it was not until the 1920s that the Minister of Health banned some colours from use. In 1957, a new list was issued, not of what was banned but of what would be permitted, namely 32 artificial colours and 13 natural ones. This list has steadily shrunk, partly to match use in other EC countries, and by 1992 will have shrunk further to a group common to all Community countries. As with flavours, more use of plant shoot and root cultures will see natural colours more widely used, but in neither case does this guarantee an end to any risk.

Food colours have been particularly linked with allergies. Dr Tom Coultate, lecturer at the South Bank Polytechnic in London and author of *Food, the Chemistry of its Components*, says 'the stringency of the toxicity testing procedures that have been applied in Britain and abroad forces the conclusion that the food colours now permitted are at least as safe as any of the more "natural" components of our diet'. But he goes on to say that such tests do not look at allergy, intolerance or hypersensitivity.

These issues were first raised in America by Dr Ben Feingold. His work on intolerance of aspirin led him to study intolerance in children, and to suggest that artificial colours and flavours in foods (as well as naturally-occurring salicylates, which are aspirin-like substances) made some children hyperactive. Many others have followed up this work, and it is now agreed that some children do indeed respond allergically to synthetic colours, above all to tartrazine. According to Coultate, the response is more likely to show up as a rash, itching or asthma than hypersensitivity, since the most rigorous studies have failed to show a significant effect of diet on behaviour. He says the total number susceptible in Britain is reckoned to fall between about 5,000 and 50,000, and these children also react to salicylates, the anti-oxidant benzoate and to other foods including cows' milk, chocolate, grapes, wheat and oranges.

This, as well as their cosmetic use, has led to widespread suspicion of colours. In fact as we have seen people who suffer intolerance are sensitive to a wide range of food ingredients and while banning tartrazine would remove one cause it would leave a large number of others. Sufferers need to know what foods are free of ingredients like wheat and its derivatives, soya and its derivatives, cocoa, BHA, BHT and benzoate, glutamate and other colours which lead to intolerance. Such information is slowly becoming available as the problems of food intolerance are more widely recognised.

The CA's assessment in *Understanding Additives* was that 'the Scientific Committee for Food (SCF – the European Community's advisory committee on food safety) estimated in 1982 that between 3 and 15 people in every 10,000 in the population may suffer reactions to food additives. MAFF estimates that for everyone who may have an adverse reaction to a food additive possibly as many as 30 or more may experience problems from foods such as milk, eggs, wheat or soya. Against this background, MAFF started a research programme in 1987 to study the incidence of adverse reactions in the general population, and the mechanisms which may be involved.

'The SCF's estimate was corroborated by the results of the MAFF study: only in a very few cases do clinically reproducible symptoms occur as a result of the consumption of additives in the amounts likely to be present in food. As part of the study, ten per cent of the population in the Wycombe Health Authority in Buckinghamshire, 30,000 people, were sent a questionnaire designed to identify those who thought that they suffered adverse reactions to additives. Eighty-one people who stated that they had a problem took part in detailed medical screening. Participants were tested with a combination of colours, preservatives, antioxidants and aspirin . Of these 81, only three people showed positive reactions. Two had adverse reactions to annato (a natural colour) and one to a cocktail of colours. This gives a percentage rate for the population of between 0.01 and 0.26 per cent, close to the low level identified by the SCF. Put another way, however, Britain's population of 56 million could include between 5,500 and 112,000 people who potentially have adverse reactions to additives in food.

'It is now generally believed that the people who react to some additives also have adverse reactions to other foods or substances. For instance, people who experience adverse reactions to aspirin seem more likely to react to certain additives.'

Other additives include emulsifiers, thickeners and stabilisers which help maintain togetherness in substances, for example oil and water in mayonnaise, which are reluctant mixers and either poor eating or something quite different when separate. As the CA puts it, 'some modern foods could not exist without additives. Salad cream would separate if emulsifiers and stabilisers were not used. Margarine requires emulsifiers and stabilisers, and had it not been coloured yellow like butter, it is questionable whether it would have been as popular as it is now. Any instant desserts, packet soups and coffee creams have complex combinations of additives to create their different characteristics. Spray cream requires a propellant to eject it from the can, while in the snack food and processed meat product areas, additives have played a substantial part in changing staple foods into a wide variety of crisps, potato products, pâtés, sausages and sliced cured meats, with different compositions and flavours.'

This brings us back to the debate about need. Dr Verner Wheelock, of the University of Bradford's department of Food Policy Research, argued in mid-1986 that many consumers were more concerned about reducing additive intake than about increasing fibre consumption or reducing fat intake. Additives in products such as low fat spreads discouraged consumers from switching to them as a sound way to reduce fat consumption.

He went on to quote from the Food Additives Campaign Team (FACT) literature. 'Most additives are the means whereby low quality ingredients, saturated fats and sugars, can be disguised as good, nutritious food. Many common additives cause a number of illnesses in vulnerable people, notably children. In addition, forty one additives approved for use in Britain are under suspicion because they may cause cancer in laboratory animals.' Wheelock commented: 'The reality is that FACT is making a mountain out of a molehill.'

The CA in their book takes a position in the middle. 'Although consumers are conscious of the need for a healthy diet, surveys have shown that their major concern is to have convenience foods to suit the family's everyday requirements.

'The vast majority of additives in use are not intended to protect public health, and may be considered cosmetic. They affect the taste, texture and appearance of foods, and arguably none of them are essential, in the sense that we can live without them, and will not become ill if they are not present. They contribute to the variety of food, and hence to people's enjoyment. It should be a matter of choice whether or not to consume them in the quantities in which they now exist.'

Wheelock and FACT effectively look at the same scene from different viewpoints. Wheelock thinks the attention paid to additives has muddled consumers, who would do much better to focus on fat and fibre. FACT thinks a clear focus on fat and fibre is made more difficult by the use of additives to tart up nutritionally unsatisfactory ingredients. But Wheelock joins FACT in criticising attitudes in today's highly competitive food industry where staff are recruited for marketing skills rather than for knowledge of food and the food industry. Marketeers have looked at additives as an opportunity or threat for their product depending on formulation – and although there are technical reasons why fewer additives are now needed, it would have been simpler never to have used many of them in the first place. He comments that past failures to respond to genuine consumer worries did nothing to enhance the industry's reputation, while the switch to removing additives undermined credibility even further.

Whether for marketing or nutritional reasons, industry continues to look closely at additives, both to limit their use and to assist consumer choice by labelling. So FACT has achieved a number of its objectives and Wheelock suggested it could now take a fresh aim. 'If its members and supporters are genuinely concerned about food safety they would be much better advised to direct their fire at those areas where there really is a need for action ... There is a pressing need to improve the hygienic standards of food handling and preparation ... There must be many cafés and restaurants which have filthy kitchens. There are numerous butchers' shops which use the same slicing machine for raw meat as for cooked meat. Yet the enforcement agencies are starved of funds and are strictly limited in the control they can exert.

'These agencies are also responsible for enforcing the regulations on additives. As their resources shrink the possibility of additive misuse will almost certainly increase . . . It would be in the interests of consumers and the responsible elements in the food industry if the laws could be properly enforced. Campaigning for such an objective would be much more worthwhile than attempting to get the existing regulations altered so that they are more restrictive.'

Since then attitudes have changed further, and now the Food Safety Bill is moving towards ensuring that the enforcement agencies do have greater powers to ensure safe food. At the same time the increasing influence of Brussels is carrying the additives' debate into a European context as it works to harmonise standards throughout the Community.

HOW GOOD FOR YOU IS THE LABEL WHICH SAYS NATURAL?

Will Waites, professor of Food Microbiology at Nottingham, told a conference organised by the Centre for Agricultural Strategy in the summer of 1989 that naturally-occurring compounds in foods are far more likely to cause toxicity than intentional food additives.

Although microbiologists have known this for at least 20 years, regulatory authorities, the media and some consumers still insist that natural toxicants are insignificant. Waites gave this list of principal ones found in the diet:

Compound	Common source
cyanogenic glucosides	legumes, fruit kernels
lectins (haemagglutinins)	legumes

protease inhibitors	legumes
glucosinolates	brassicas
biogenic amines	cheese, chocolate, wine
lathyrogens	chickpea
favogenic factors	fava beans
alkaloids	herbal teas
glycoalkaloids	potatoes
phytoestrogens	legumes
saponins	legumes
tannins	widespread
psoralens	umbelliferae (carrot, etc)
terpenes	widespread
ptaquiloside	goats milk (via bracken)

He pointed out that many of these can survive processing and cooking and relatively few had received a fraction of the toxicological evaluation devoted to synthetic food additives and contaminants. Changes in eating habits had produced new risks like the recent cases of poisoning from kidney bean lectins. Developments in both the direct consumption of cereals, vegetables and fruit, and in food processing technology which would increase their availability and palatability, would mean more of these foods were eaten and he said that 'studies in this area are required and the situation needs to be kept under constant review.

'An example of the increased intake which has been noted is that of vegetarians. For omnivores in the UK, the mean daily intakes of saponins and oestrogenic isoflavone glycosides are about 20mg and less than 1mg respectively, whereas in vegetarians the corresponding figures are more than 200mg and more than 100mg respectively.

'There has also been a recent increase in the popularity of potato skins, especially in the form of baked potatoes. This is likely to lead to an increase in the consumption of glykoalkaloids such as chaconine and solanine.

Recent work has suggested that these compounds can increase the permeability of gastrointestinal cells to other non-nutritive food constituents. However, the significance of this for man is unknown.

'Pyrrolizidialkaloids are also acutely toxic and have led to human fatalities. Since these are present in "health-foods" such as herbal teas and some plant materials taken as dietary supplements there is the possibility that the prolonged intake of such compounds could present future problems.'

Dr Roger Fenwick, of the Institute of Food Research in Norwich has looked at some of the half million or more chemical compounds found naturally in plants. His work supports Waites's conclusion that we shall need to know more about the chemicals found naturally in plants.

Thus the glycoalkaloids in potatoes interfere with the normal function of the central nervous system and irritate the gut. They are found in the largest amounts in above ground parts like leaves, but also in the skin, so peeling potatoes reduces the glycoalkaloid content greatly. One new potato cultivar, Lenape, has already been withdrawn from the market in North America because under the growing conditions of the north eastern states it was found to be toxic. Fenwick says that 'acute illnesses, and even death, in animals and man have followed the consumption of damaged, rotten, green, sprouted or blighted potatoes – that is, low quality, sub-standard produce . . . The most recent outbreak of potato poisoning occurred ten years ago in Lewisham. Seventy eight school boys were taken ill . . . seventeen required hospital treatment with three being described as seriously ill . . .

'If it were to be seriously suggested that compounds with the biological activity of glycoalkaloids should be added to any food, let alone such a staple one as potatoes, there would be considerable, and justified, concern.'

He gives brassicas as another example. They contain

glucosinolates which break down into a range of products. One group, the indoles, has been shown to be anti-carcinogenic and may help protect against human gastric and other cancers; but indoles also react with nitrite to form nitrosamines which have been considered to act as carcinogens in animals and man.

Legumes contain saponins as well as a 'wide range of additional toxicants, including tannins, oligosaccharides, phytate, lectins, enzyme inhibitors and oestrogenic isoflavones, and the effect of the saponins may be to increase the absorption of these molecules and hence their biological activity . . . The presence in soya and its products particularly, of large amounts of isoflavones and coumestans having obvious oestrogenic effects may also be significant. Preliminary studies have shown that whilst the population at large has a mean daily intake of such compounds below 1mg, that of vegetarians may be 100mg or more.' Vegetarians are likely to eat double the amount of glucosinolates, from five to ten times that of glycoalkaloids and perhaps five times as much saponins.

Fenwick points out that as plant breeders aim for greater resistance to pests and diseases so these chemicals, which are produced by the plant for defensive reasons, will increase. Further, some of them are produced in response to injury or attack both before and after harvest; where less or no chemical protection is used, levels of these compounds are likely to rise. But he stresses that our ignorance of the detailed biology of nutrition is such that nobody knows what the effects may be. 'Natural compounds in the diet may be both beneficial and deleterious, what is needed is to gain a wide knowledge of possible effects so that these may be included in any risk assessment or dietary benefit analysis. In many cases it is likely to be the overall balance of biological activity which will be important.'

Both he and Waites confirm the general acceptance

among food scientists that food additives should be ranked in the lowest risk category, a conclusion first reached as long ago as 1971 by the Director of the Bureau of Foods in the Food and Drug Administration (FDA), Dr V. O. Wodicka. He put the dangers from our food in this order:

    microbiological
    nutritional environmental contaminants (pollutants)
    natural toxicants
    pesticide residues
    food additives.

In 1978, Howard Roberts, also of the FDA, looked at the same subject in a slightly different way. This was his ranking of the dangers:

    foodborne hazards of microbial origin
    malnutrition
    environmental contaminants
    mycotoxins and natural toxicants
    food additives.

Both agreed that environmental and natural toxicants were 100 times as risky as additives and pesticide residues, and that microbes and malnutrition were 1,000 times more risky again.

Beyond all these worries is the fear of cancer. The Sherlock Holmes of the causes of cancer is Professor Sir Richard Doll. In 1981 he and his colleague Richard Peto (an equal partner, not the amiable but bumbling fall guy Dr Watson was to the great detective) published a report on the *Causes of Cancer*. Food additives were estimated to cause less than 1% of all deaths from cancer, with a possible range from minus 5% to 2%. This compares with a best estimate of 35% of all cancer deaths which may be caused by diet, with a possible range (showing clearly how uncertain the scientific data are) from 10% to 70%. The possible minus value for additives is due to benefits from preservatives, mentioned above.

This well-known study was commissioned by the US Congress Office of Technology Assessment, but there is no reason to think the results would be different here and in much of Europe. Indeed, in a recent overview of the evidence linking diet and cancer (to be published by the Nutrition Society during 1990) Doll has confirmed this. He writes: 'There is now uniform agreement among oncologists (people who study cancer) that the incidence of cancer is determined, in large part, by factors in the environment and aspects of behaviour that are capable of modification or avoidance. It is agreed, too, that by such means the age-specific incidence of the disease in middle and old age could be reduced by some 80-90 per cent. That the proportion should be so high should not be surprising, when it is borne in mind that we now know some 50 causes of human cancer that are responsible, between them, for some 40 per cent of all cancers that occur annually throughout the world, while in this country tobacco alone is responsible for about a third of all cancer deaths. It may be surprising, however, that diet is also commonly suggested to be responsible for some 30-70 per cent of the total, when so few aspects of diet have been established as causes of the disease.

'This figure of 30-70 per cent is, in fact, a guess based partly on the knowledge that the diet of experimental animals has a major influence on the incidence of cancer produced by treatment with a variety of laboratory carcinogens, and partly on the simplistic belief that what you put into your mouth and pass through the digestive tract is likely to play a large part in the production of cancers of the corresponding organs which, in Britain, are responsible for 30 per cent of all cancers.

'That up to 70 per cent has been thought to be possibly attributable to diet should not, however, be surprising when it is borne in mind that the production of cancer is a process, the progress of which may be influenced by many factors, and that the avoidance of each factor individually can have the same final effect. We can, therefore, properly say that two factors may each be responsible for (say) 80 to 90 per cent of the risk of developing a particular type of the disease, while the avoidance of both will have little more effect than the avoidance of one ... It is quite possible, therefore, that dietary modification could help to reduce the incidence of cancers that are now known to be due to tobacco, occupational hazards, viral infection, ultra-violet light, and ionizing radiation, even if these hazards continue to exist unchanged. This should not, of course, be an excuse for not reducing hazards that are capable of control, particularly when many of them can be controlled more easily and at less social expense than would be involved by major changes in the national diet. It does, however, explain how we can talk about diet being responsible for up to 70 per cent of the risk of cancer when more than 30 per cent is certainly attributable to other causes.'

Professor Doll thus emphasises that although there is much evidence linking diet with cancer, it remains difficult to offer detailed and specific dietary advice because the interactions are so complex.

He identifies four established causes, obesity (and rapid growth in childhood), aflatoxin, alcohol and the consumption of salted fish by southern Chinese. Suspected causes, he says, are legion and include eating too much of possibly harmful foods and too little of probably protective foods. Thus much eating of fat and meat, and not enough of fruit, vegetables, vitamins, trace elements and fibre (or complex starches) have all been linked to certain cancers. So far, the evidence has been insufficient to shift such suspects confidently over to the group of established causes.

Non-nutrient chemicals, both natural and synthetic, found in food may have either harmful or beneficial consequences. 'Methods of food preservation could be important . . . but I know of no worthwhile evidence to suggest that any additives, other than those used for preservation, or any contaminant of food, such as pesticide residues, which have given rise to so much public concern, have been responsible for any hazard large enough to be detectable.'

Professor Doll concludes that some, but not all, of these aspects of diet will prove to be causes of disease. But, he says, 'how we can become certain enough about their effects to provide people with adequate information for them to make a sensible balance of the benefits and risks of particular ways of life still, unfortunately, presents a difficult problem for nutritionists of all sorts.'

Although precisely the same problem afflicts Americans, they took a different approach over 30 years ago, through the well-known Delaney clause. In principle straightforward and apparently sensible, it became American law in 1959, and said that no substance which caused cancer in animals could be added to food.

In 1984, Edith Efron in her book *The Apocalyptics* spelt out the difficulty of Delaney for the FDA which regulates what Americans swallow. She quoted Bruce Ames, chairman of the Department of Biochemical Medicine at the University of California, Berkeley and a molecular biologist with a long history in cancer research and in regulating industrial chemicals.

'In a literature review in *Science*, Ames informed the world that nature was not benign, that the natural food supply was full of an extraordinary number of complex and toxic chemicals, that there were so many carcinogens and mutagens and genotoxic substances in the natural diet that one could eat no meal without consuming them; indeed that there were so many that he could discuss only a few examples. The ones he named were those he considered most important by virtue of their potency and the quantity consumed.

'Inevitably, his list included the Japanese discoveries that cooked, browned and burned proteins, amino acids and sugars were mutagenic and carcinogenic. He also reported that oxidised fats and cooking oils were mutagenic and carcinogenic, (and) that their potency increased in the cooking process . . . In addition, he reported that carcinogenic nitroso-compounds could be formed by eating a host of nitrate-rich vegetables; that such spices as black pepper and such foods as mushrooms contained powerful carcinogens; that commonplace vegetables and fruits and generally plant foods contained carcinogens and mutagens . . . ; that various natural molds added their potent carcinogenicity to a great variety of plant and animal foods; that the mutagen and co-carcinogen acetaldehyde was produced by the human body in the course of metabolising liquor; that coffee was mutagenic; that coffee, tea and chocolate were genotoxic . . .

'How did Ames calculate the risks for so great an array of natural carcinogens, mutagens and genotoxic substances? He didn't. Risk assessment would, he said, constitute a major challenge.'

Since then the point has frequently been made that if all food was subjected to this sort of risk assessment much of what we eat would be banned. Indeed, in 1979 four years before Ames wrote his paper, two legal advisers to the FDA, Peter Hutt and Richard Merrill, had already written: 'A requirement of warnings on all foods that may contain an inherent carcinogenic ingredient or a carcinogenic contaminant (in contrast to a deliberately added carcinogenic substance) would apply to many, perhaps most, foods in a supermarket. Such warnings would be so numerous they would confuse the public, would not promote informed consumer decision-making, and would not advance the public health.'

Professor Ames has since faced the challenge of trying to calculate the risks. He and a team summarised the evidence in an article called Ranking Possible Carcinogenic Hazards, published in *Science*, April 1987. The introduction admits however that while the ranking suggests that carcinogenic hazards from current levels of pesticide residues or water pollution are likely to be of minimal concern relative to the background levels of natural substances, we do not know whether these natural exposures are likely to be of major or minor importance.

Ames stresses that the calculations of these rankings, which link human contact with chemicals to their potency in animal tests, can be no more than a guide, in part because of the uncertainties in using rats to predict risks in humans. 'Extrapolation from the results of rodent cancer tests done at high doses to effects on humans exposed to low doses is routinely attempted by regulatory agencies when formulating policies attempting to prevent future cancer. There is little sound scientific basis for this type of extrapolation . . . Nevertheless, to be prudent in regulatory policy, and in the absence of good human data (almost always the case), some reliance on animal cancer tests is unavoidable. The best use of them should be made even though few, if any, of the main avoidable causes of human cancer have typically been the types of man-made chemicals that are being tested in animals . . . There is increasing evidence that our normal diet contains many rodent carcinogens, all perfectly natural or traditional (for example, from the cooking of food), and that no human diet can be free of mutagens or agents that can be carcinogenic in rodent systems. We need to identify the important causes of human cancer among the vast number of minimal risks.'

That is difficult, both because of the uncertainties with rodent tests and because few natural chemicals have been tested at all. Despite the difficulties, Ames has produced numbers, and in what follows his assessment of the possible risk from ordinary (American) tap water is taken as a baseline and all other risks are related to that.

Pesticide residues in America (including residues of industrial chemicals like polychlorinated biphenyls – PCBs) in food average 150 μg/day (one μg or microgram is one millionth of a gram). 'Most (105 μg) of this intake is composed of three chemicals (ethylhexyl diphenyl phosphate, malathion and chlorpropham) shown to be non-carcinogenic in tests on rodents.'

Three man-made chemicals found in food which may increase the risk of cancer are PCBs, DDE/DDT and EDB (ethylene dibromide). Tap water is, respectively, five times, three times and two-and-a-half times more risky than these three chemicals when swallowed in food. Ames says that 'the average US daily intake of DDE from DDT is equivalent to the (risk from) the chloroform in one glass of tapwater and thus appears to be insignificant compared to the background of natural carcinogens in our diet. Even daily consumption of 100 times the average intake of DDE/DDT or PCBs would produce a possible hazard that is small compared to other common exposures . . . '

He contrasts this with natural pesticides. 'We are ingesting in our diet at least 10,000 times more by weight of natural pesticides than of man-made pesticide residues. These are natural "toxic chemicals" that have an enormous variety of chemical structures, appear to be present in all plants, and serve to protect plants against fungi, insects and animal predators . . . There has been relatively little interest in the toxicology or carcinogenicity of these compounds until quite recently, although they are by far the main source of "toxic chemicals" ingested by humans. Only a few dozen of the thousands present in the human diet have been tested in animal bioassays . . . A sizable proportion of those that have been tested are carcinogens, and many others have been shown to be mutagens, so it is probable that many more will be found to be carcinogens if tested.'

He lists symphytine from comfrey, allyl isothiocyanate from brown mustard, estragole from basil, hydrazines from mushrooms and safrole from root beer. At an average daily dose (for example, one cup of comfrey tea) they are respectively 30, 70, 100, 100, and 200 times as risky as a glass of tap water. If the symphytine is consumed as a comfrey tablet, it can be more than 1,000 times riskier than tap water.

A considerable percentage of moulds tested have proved to be mutagens and carcinogens. Some are highly potent. The mould aflatoxin can infect peanuts, wheat, maize, other nuts and a wide variety of stored carbohydrates. Ames calculates the risk from the aflatoxin content of a single peanut butter sandwich as 30 times that of a glass of tapwater. 'Considering the potency of those mold toxins that have been tested and the widespread contamination of food with molds, they may represent the most significant carcinogenic pollution of the food supply in developing countries. Such pollution is much less severe in industrialized countries, due to refrigeration and modern techniques of agriculture and storage, including use of synthetic pesticides and fumigants.'

Boozers will be unhappy to hear of the risks of alcohol in Ames's rankings. A glass of beer is nearly 3,000, a glass of wine nearly 5,000 times as risky as a glass of tap water. 'The possible hazard of alcohol is enormous relative to that from the intake of synthetic chemical residues.' Bread eaters will be shaken to hear that the formaldehyde present in a sandwich is on these calculations 400 times riskier than a glass of tap water; but Ames points out that we generate formaldehyde metabolically from substances which we eat in plants and there are thus high levels found normally in human blood, so detoxification mechanisms must be important.

He confirms the risks of cooking, with nine compounds which occur with heating proteins and amino acids shown to be potent carcinogens in rodents. Even breathing has its risks, since the air in the average home contains enough formaldehyde to make it 600 times riskier than what comes out of the tap. But cooks should know that 'the total amount of browned and burnt material eaten in a typical day is at least several hundred times more than that inhaled from severe air pollution' – and anyone who lives in a house that 'indoor air pollution is, in general, worse than outdoor air pollution, partly because of cigarette smoke. One must breathe Los Angeles smog for a year to inhale the same amount of burnt material that a smoker (two packs) inhales in a day . . .'

Ames, who has continued to assess the hazards of industrial and natural chemicals, emphasises that the point of his article is not to worry people about eating mushrooms or drinking wine, but 'to put the possible risks of man-made carcinogens in proper perspective and to point out that we lack the knowledge to do low-dose "risk assessment". We also are almost completely ignorant of the carcinogenic potential of the enormous background of natural chemicals in the world . . .

'The idea that nature is benign and that evolution has allowed us to cope perfectly with the toxic chemicals in the natural world is not compelling for several reasons.' He has recently taken to joking that plants devote the same efforts to defence as humans. Around 7% of their energy goes on defence, and around 7% of Gross National Product is spent by developed countries for the same reason.

He gives just one example of the consequence of failure to grasp these realities. 'An EPA "risk assessment" based on a succession of worst case assumptions concluded that EDB residues in grain could cause three cases of cancer in 1,000 people. A consequence was the banning of the main fumigant in the country. It would have been more reasonable to compare the possible hazard of EDB residues to that of other common possible hazards. For example, the aflatoxin in the average peanut butter sandwich, or a raw mushroom, are 75, and 200 times, respectively, the possible hazard of EDB. Before banning EDB, a useful substance with rather low residue levels, it might be reasonable to consider whether the hazards of the alternatives, such as food irradiation, or the consequences of banning, such as increased mold contamination of grain, pose less risk to society.'

He repeats his conclusion that levels of synthetic pollutants in drinking water and of synthetic pesticide residues in foods are likely to be minimal carcinogenic hazards relative to the background of natural carcinogens. 'Obviously, prudence is desirable with regard to pollution, but we do need to work out some balance between chemophobia with its high costs to the national wealth, and sensible management of industrial chemicals.'

That balance is a long way off at present. Efron summarised the difficulty when she said that 'the plain but astonishing fact was that by 1979, twenty years after the passage of the famous Delaney Clause which forbids the inclusion of carcinogens in foods, the FDA, as a matter of policy, was refusing to warn the American people, so as not to "confuse" them, that much if not most of their food supply was contaminated with natural carcinogens or was intrinsically carcinogenic itself. The reason, said Merrill, was obvious. "The number of carcinogenic substances that naturally occur in foods would ultimately require so many warnings as to be deafening." Thus, the agency would only warn the public of "deliberately added" carcinogens, and an enormous and growing literature of experiments reporting carcinogens and mutagens in natural foods was being officially ignored.'

In practice, this makes Delaney the Mr Canute of cancer prevention. Faced with what was seen as a rising tide of cancer-causing chemicals created by industry, Delaney told it to turn back. He got wet feet from the large number of natural carcinogens in food.

When King Canute told the tide to turn back it was to show his courtiers the limits of our power over nature. When Mr Canute did so, it was to show our power over industry. Efron allowed herself some elbow room to describe 'the hypocritical double standard for industry and for nature. The public will learn that the story that cancer was invented in . . . test tubes is false. The public will learn that it has been taught myths about the planet. The public will discover that the cancer "preventers" have been brandishing industrial perils at them while declining to inform them of the natural. The public will discover why "the richest, longest-lived, best protected, most resourceful civilisation, with the highest degree of insight into its own technology, is on its way to becoming the most frightened".'

There is no Delaney clause as such in Europe, although there are a good number of home-grown Canutes with wet feet. But if there really is a sea of dangerous natural chemicals in our food, how are the rest of us to keep afloat and why didn't we all drown long ago?

It is because the risks from these substances are very small. Sir Donald Acheson estimated the risks of dying from an accident in the home were 100 times greater than of dying from salmonella food poisoning. If, as suggested by Wodicka, food poisoning is about 1,000 times more risky than natural toxicants in food, then one is about 100,000 times more likely to die from an accident in the home than from the toxicants which Ames and others describe. And if, as Wodicka also suggests, natural toxicants are 100 times more risky than food additives and pesticides, then one is about 10 million times more likely to die from an accident in the home than from these chemicals. However speculative these numbers – which they unquestionably are – they give an idea of the risks involved.

Let us leave the last word with the British Medical Association. 'Doll and Peto have estimated that around 35% of all cancer deaths in the United States could be attributed to dietary factors, but they do emphasise that this figure is highly speculative and chiefly refers to factors in the diet which have not yet been reliably identified . . . There are many indications that diet can be of great importance in determining the risk of cancers of the stomach and intestinal tract and some cancers of the female sex organs, but as yet, there is little firm evidence on which conclusions can be based. It is probable that the most important factors will turn out to be those related to nutrition as a whole, including the total balance of the diet, the presence of vitamins and minerals, and other microscopic elements of the normal diet which may either enhance or inhibit the formation of cancer. Less likely to be important is the ingestion of tiny traces of powerful carcinogens which to most people are the main source of worry . . .

'Further, it is important to consider the benefits of food additives as well as their risks. While the benefits of flavouring and colouring additives may in many cases be questionable, it has been argued that the use of chemical preservatives has substantially reduced the risk of cancer overall, knowing as we do the carcinogenic potential of older methods of food preservation such as pickling, smoking and curing . . .

'In the last 50 years the only cancer which has increased dramatically in incidence is cancer of the lung, and that has happened in both sexes . . . While lung cancers have increased in incidence, two types of cancer which have shown a steady decline in the same period are those of the uterus and the stomach ... Apart from lung, stomach and uterine cancer, the incidence of most cancers has stayed about the same for the last 30 years.'

CHAPTER SIX:

How safe are New Technologies? Food Irradiation and BST

Radiant energy comes in very different shapes and sizes. We usually meet it as light and heat and that's how we think about it, but we could think of it instead as super-tankers and jet fighters – in other words, a range from very large and slow to very small and fast. At the large slow end are radio waves, at the small, fast end are X rays and gamma rays. Light is somewhere around the middle of this range, perhaps in our analogy filling the space occupied by commercial transport like buses and lorries. The full range of radiant energy is called the electromagnetic spectrum.

When any of these forms of energy strikes matter, heating occurs. The commonest everyday experience of this is the warmth of sunlight (or an electric fire) on the skin. Cooks use this heating to change the structure of food. Another such change in structure comes from using gamma rays, which is what happens when food is irradiated. And microwaves can be used in a similar way to pasteurise food by briefly raising internal temperatures to kill most micro-organisms.

Low dose irradiation slows down the ripening and

sprouting of fruit and vegetables, and kills pests, such as insects present after harvesting. For example, it is used instead of growth-suppressing chemicals to slow sprouting in potatoes, or in cereal grains instead of chemical insecticides to kill storage pests. Medium doses kill bacteria and reduce the dangers of food poisoning. For example, it is used to kill bacteria which contaminate shellfish. High doses sterilise food completely and are used by hospitals for patients who need a completely sterile diet.

Food irradiation was first used in 1921, and in 1930 a French patent was granted on the process. In the UK, intensive research on irradiation started in 1948 and went on for over 15 years. Despite assurances by scientists that it was safe, the government banned it in 1964, except for use in hospital diets.

In 1970, an international food irradiation programme was started in West Germany, financed by 19 countries of which the UK was one. Largely as a result, a joint expert committee of the United Nations concluded that the process presented no toxicological hazard and introduced no special nutritional or microbiological problems. It confirmed this view in 1980. It said: 'The irradiation of any food commodity up to an overall dose of 10kGy (a measure of radiation equivalent to the medium dose level described above) presents no toxicological hazard; hence, toxicological testing of foods so treated is no longer required.' The Codex Alimentarius Commission of the World Health Organisation (WHO) adopted this conclusion in 1983.

In 1981 WHO reported again. 'Evidence from most studies suggests that in the low dose range (up to 1kGy) used for irradiation of food, nutrient losses are insignificant. In the medium range (1kGy to 10kGy) losses of some vitamins may occur, if air is not excluded during irradiation and storage. At high doses, technology is such that losses may be less than at medium doses.' But WHO said that the importance of these losses is linked to the place of the food in question in the complete diet, so each food needs to be considered separately. For example, both fish and chicken lose vitamin B1 after irradiation; in the UK, both contribute little B1 to the diet, but in a culture where eating fish contributed significant amounts of B1, irradiation of fish could be detrimental.

In 1988 WHO summed up its attitudes in its publication on *Food Irradiation*. Food is irradiated for the same reasons that it is processed by heat or refrigeration or freezing or treated with chemicals – to kill insects, fungi and bacteria that cause food to spoil and can cause disease, and to make it possible to keep it longer and in better condition in warehouses, stores and homes. It also said that the treatment does not alter the food in any way that could harm people, and that food irradiated under approved conditions does not become radio-active. But like other methods of treatment it could lower the content of some nutrients, such as vitamins. At low doses of radiation, nutrient losses were either not measurable or were not significant. At the higher doses used to extend shelf-life or control harmful bacteria, nutritional losses were less than, or about the same as, those caused by other kinds of food processing. It can, claimed WHO, certainly be said that irradiated foods were wholesome and nutritious.

Further, studies in animals conducted by reputable organisations in many different countries and often continued for periods of years had disclosed no reason to be concerned about long-term health effects of irradiated food or about risks from eating such food.

'Over the last 30 years, many hundreds of tests have been carried out with animals fed irradiated foods . . . A very small number of these tests gave inconclusive results that were interpreted as showing that food irradiation is unsafe. Each of these studies has been thoroughly reviewed and, in many cases, repeated. The results of these follow-up investigations provided explanations for the original "negative" findings. Usually the problem lay in the design of the study or the way it was conducted. Sometimes the sample size – the number of animals used in the study – was too small to allow the results to be interpreted properly. In other instances, the repeat studies were simply unable to reproduce the original results. In fact, more than 100 generations of sensitive laboratory animals in the United Kingdom alone have been living and prospering on diets sterilised by irradiation. Similar results have been obtained in many other countries.'

WHO went on to consider the chemicals, known as 'radiolytic' products, formed in food which has been irradiated and said, 'such compounds are formed in food processed by radiation and they are identical or similar to compounds found in food processed by other techniques, such as cooking, or even in unprocessed foods. Extensive research has been done to identify and evaluate radiolytic products in food. No one can say with certainty that all such products have been found, but the important finding is that all those identified so far are similar to compounds commonly found in food. They are not unique in the sense that they occur only as a result of irradiation. And, moreover, there is no evidence that any of these substances poses a danger to human health . . .

'Chemicals and other agents capable of damaging cells are called mutagens. Our food, irradiated or not, naturally contains some mutagens. They can be formed by conventional food processing methods whose safety is accepted. Smoked foods, for example, may contain chemicals that can injure cells. But, despite extensive studies, there is no evidence that irradiated foods present any increased risk of exposure to mutagens.'

In 1982 the British government set up the Advisory Committee on Irradiated and Novel Foods (ACINF) to look at the problem once more. It published its report in 1986 and advised that, under specified controls, irradiation was a safe and useful food preservation technology.

The National Consumer Council (NCC) responded in detail to the ACINF Report. It said that concern was fully understandable, but that consumers must accept some form of food treatment if they expected perishable foods to survive production, transportation, storage and display, prior to purchase.

'Food irradiation is essentially an alternative method of preserving and maintaining the quality of food. It can eliminate or reduce spoilage caused by micro-organisms, insects and sprouting without the need for chemical treatment. It is also the only reliable way of eliminating salmonella . . .

'In a recent letter, the Director of the Public Health Laboratory Service stated that he estimates that about 80% of frozen chickens on sale in supermarkets are contaminated with salmonella, although he adds that there is no significant risk to the consumer if the chickens are adequately thawed and properly cooked. Nevertheless, any process which promises to eliminate salmonella in certain products is deserving of serious consideration.'

On vitamin losses the NCC stressed that the effects of irradiation on the nutrient content of total diet must be closely monitored, particularly among at risk groups, such as infants, children and pregnant women. A further worry was the possibility of adverse interaction between additives and food which had been irradiated. More information might also be needed about possible risks from contamination of irradiated foods by wrapping materials.

Thus the NCC accepted the basic safety of the process as well as its potential contribution to food preservation but raised questions about a number of side effects and possible abuses. It insisted that tight controls – over labelling, suitability on a product-by-product basis, use of tests to show whether food has been irradiated, guarantees that only fresh foods are processed – must be central to any system which was put in place. When these conditions were met, the NCC would accept its introduction, but stressed that 'we have still to be convinced that sufficient information exists to be reasonably sure that irradiation does not pose any new hazards to the consumer'.

Other consumer groups have expressed similar views. The European Bureau of Consumers' Unions (BEUC) and the Consumers in the European Community Group (CECG) both want a much closer look at any long-term effects, close control of procedures, and restriction of the process to foods difficult to preserve otherwise or which use fumigation chemicals like ethylene oxide. *Which?* said: 'Overall our survey suggests that if food irradiation were to be permitted in this country, food manufacturers might have considerable difficulty in selling it.' It also concluded that consumers are confused about the process.

The British Medical Association (BMA) also responded to the ACINF report. In March 1987 it said: 'The Board believes that the current advice . . . may not sufficiently take account of, still less exclude, possible long-term medical effects on the population, given that "irradiated" products have been available for a relatively short period of time. More scientific data is required, . . and the Board therefore believes that a full-scale study should be undertaken, in collaboration with the medical associations of those countries where the process is already in use. Such a study is necessary before the process can be confidently accepted in this country . . .' It may be that the BMA does not speak with one voice on the subject, however. In its excellent book *Infection Control* published in 1989 the authors discuss salmonella contamination of foods and say: 'Protein feedstuffs should be sterilised, and all cows' milk products pasteurised. But in the case of poultry, it may be that the only way to ensure that the carcases are not infected at the point of sale is to irradiate them at the processing plant.'

Another recent assessment of the virtues and vices of irradiation has come from Helen Blackholly and Paul Thomas of Bradford University's Food Policy Research Unit. Like many others, they point out that irradiation is not a blanket answer to food preservation. Each food must be considered separately to see how suitable it is for the technology and to work out the right dose for the job.

For example, low dose irradiation is used to stop mangoes getting over-ripe but apples need a higher dose and suffer from increased softening as a result. Some fruit and vegetables may change taste as well as texture. High-fat foods can become rancid. Excess levels of treatment can alter colour, flavour and texture, and where that happens the technique is unsuitable. It can be difficult to use for controlling fungal infection, and more needs to be known about doses and survival rates of moulds before irradiation will be a good way to cope with them.

They stress that food must be fresh when it is irradiated. If not, there is a danger that microbial poisons may have accumulated so that, although the microbes themselves are killed, the poison is left. Botulism is an example. But using irradiation would not remove the existing controls which have reduced the dangers of botulism to very low levels. And they say that irradiation of low quality produce that smells bad does not remove the bad smell – so food which is far gone cannot easily be camouflaged. Geoffrey Campbell-Platt, professor of food technology at the University of Reading, endorses this view that irradiation cannot be used to mask food that is unfit to eat. "If food is spoiled before it is irradiated it will still appear spoiled. Food irradiation can't make bad food good," he says.

These assertions are true where spoilage is obvious.

But where bacterial contamination is not yet obvious by smell or appearance, food can be 'cleaned up' and passed off as fresh.

Blackholly and Thomas point out that measurements of vitamin loss have been in conflict, which makes it hard to get a clear picture of just what is involved. Thus three different laboratories reached three different conclusions on vitamin C losses in stored potatoes which had been irradiated. And, while overall losses may be similar to those found in canned food, it is often easier to add vitamins back to cans. A particular worry is that losses of vitamins could affect low income families most harshly, one reason why any decision on the value of the process must relate to the specific conditions under which it might be used. Campbell-Platt has said that 'the amount of nutritional loss by irradiating food is similar to that which fresh peas lose after they have been kept for several days and cooked'. He added that 'the free radicals that arise during irradiation also arise when non-irradiated food is cooked . . . All methods of food processing, including freezing and pasteurisation, affect food in all these ways'.

Blackholly and Thomas then consider the legal position. Irradiation is already used in six EEC states so that, whatever the views in this country, the Community's attitude to irradiation is important. The free movement of goods after 1992 will mean that other people's irradiated food could not be kept out, but even now it is debatable whether the UK could prevent entry of irradiated foods if anyone pursued a case to the European Court.

The Food Safety Bill which will be passed during 1990 plans to legalise irradiation in this country, and the EEC's decision is also expected then and will be made by qualified majority voting of the Council of Ministers. New directives must get 54 out of a total of 76 votes to pass. The six countries already allowing irradiation – France, Italy,

Spain, Holland, Belgium and Denmark – between them have 41 votes so could not vote through an EEC-wide directive on their own. The UK has 10 votes and thus one other country must support the directive for it to pass.

If and when radiation is allowed, it will not be widely used. Consumer groups, we have seen, are cautious. So are the supermarkets. Marks & Spencer, for example, is concerned about the lack of tests for irradiation, and the possibility of the process being used to clean-up second-rate food and disguise poor manufacturing processes. It already exerts strong control over manufacture and distribution to sustain its policy of selling fresh food of high quality and sees no need for irradiated foods as part of that policy.

Sainsbury's has taken a slightly different line. Lord Sainsbury, whose retailing nose is more tungsten-tipped than most, told the House of Lords that the great weight of international scientific opinion believed irradiation to be safe but that he also believed that the consumer ruled. 'No food retailer or manufacturer will sell irradiated food unless they find there is a consumer demand or consumer advantage. But we should not deny the opportunity to those who wish at some time in the future to buy food they believe is safer because it is irradiated.'

Manufacturers are similarly cautious. Blackholly and Thomas write: 'The British Frozen Food Federation summarise industry attitudes: "Food irradiation should not be legalised until a simple test, which indicated whether irradiation has been applied is generally available. The strictest regulatory monitoring system should be in place before legalisation, to ensure that food irradiation is never used to conceal or compensate for poor quality or for poor hygiene standards in food processing . . . All irradiated foodstuffs need to be labelled as 'irradiated' in clear and unambiguous terms at the point of sale" . . .'

The British Poultry Federation believes that the industry is already devoting considerable resources to ensuring the highest standards of hygienic practice at every level of processing and production and that there is no current evidence that consumers would find irradiation an additional reassurance on health and hygiene grounds.

'It is for these reasons that the British Poultry Federation is unlikely to support the use of irradiation in poultry. However, should there be substantial consumer or retailer demand for irradiated poultry, the British Poultry Federation would review the situation.'

The Bradford team therefore concludes that 'the market . . . likely to adopt irradiation most readily (and ultimately achieve consumer acceptance) will be that of the raw materials and ingredients industries. For example, it will be far easier to irradiate selected ingredients such as spices or herbs to be used in a ready-prepared lasagne dish and then market this to the consumer, than to try and market an irradiated lasagne dish. The direct retail market will be by far the most difficult to penetrate.'

The process will not be cheap, which will further restrict its use. It may be limited to high-value products such as certain fruits, or ones which are low in value but available in large amounts for long processing runs. Detailed cost analysis may limit sharply the opportunities for using the technology. These costs will be added to by the need for strict control, monitoring and labelling of irradiated foods. Testing for irradiation will also be needed, and however this is finally achieved the costs again will be high.

Dr Bevan Moseley of the Institute of Food Research in Reading puts it like this. 'All food will be inspected before it is irradiated and numbered before it leaves so that it can be traced. Policing will be relatively straightforward, at least at the beginning, because high capital costs for irradiation plant and consumer resistance will slow the pace of the introduction of irradiation.'

The way the technology is used will come from an assessment of risks, costs and benefits. A good statement of one possible outcome came from the recently published report of the Richmond Committee on the Microbiological Safety of Food. It said: 'The irradiation process is capable of destroying pathogenic microorganisms in food. It is practicable to apply it to poultry. Though the process is widely regarded as safe, we feel it would be wrong to seek to improve the microbiological quality of poultry meat by relying on compulsory irradiation. There is a danger that it could be used to mask bad practice and so inhibit the development of the hygienic practices we are seeking to promote in this report. We think, though, that there may be sectors of the market that would wish to choose irradiated poultry. If irradiated poultry were to become available it must be clearly labelled . . .'

When, as seems all but certain, the process is licensed here the debate will continue in the public arena – but the decisions about it will switch to those taken by consumers in the market place.

BST – PINTAS AND POLITICS

Bovine somatotropin (BST) is another name for bovine growth hormone. Its ability to increase milk production in dairy cows has become the focus of vigorous, even violent, debate. Its importance is less what it is than how it's made commercially. It is the first of a new generation of possible genetically engineered products. What happens to BST will influence biotechnology.

The companies, all American, who make BST offer it as a cost-effective way of increasing milk ouput: production will be more efficient and so cheaper. Critics say there is too much milk in Europe and America and that producing more will be unwelcome to dairy farmers and their cows.

There are three central questions about BST. What is it? Is it safe? Why use it?

BST is a protein hormone like, for example, insulin. It is not a steroid hormone like the growth-promoting oestrogen and progesterone discussed earlier. It is produced naturally by cows in the process of metabolic control over tissue formation. The more BST a cow produces the more milk she makes, and a major genetic quality in high-yielding cows is that they naturally produce high levels of BST. When additional BST is injected, cows produce more milk. Although this has been known for over 50 years, it was very expensive to extract BST from the glands of slaughtered cattle. Thus price and any possible commercial pie both stayed sky high, until they fell to earth together in the 1970s when biotechnology worked out how to produce somatotropin cheaply. That, in turn, offered a way of producing milk more cheaply.

BST's safety is not in serious question. Consumer groups, bureacracies like the Food and Drug Administration (FDA) in America, and massive amounts of scientific evidence agree – though we shall look at one dissenting claim in some detail.

Rachel Waterhouse of the Consumers' Association has said: 'We accept that BST is safe. Certainly in the short-term, we see no problems about it.'

The FDA wrote to Congressman Peter Smith – who wanted to know why BST-treated milk was not withdrawn from circulation, and whether it was safe – on August 4, 1988. It began by explaining that, early in the investigation of any new animal drug, sponsors request authorisation from FDA to carry out research with the drug and to allow consumption of resulting food products, if appropriate after a specific withdrawal period. They had to provide the scientific evidence to support such a request, which was reviewed by the FDA to decide what withdrawal period would stop harmful residues in the food products. 'This is the typical procedure for the investigational use of new animal drugs, and BST was not an exception. Because of the safety of the milk and meat from BST-treated cows, a "zero-withdrawal" was granted. Milk and meat from BST-treated cows are safe for human consumption and FDA has allowed these food products from test herds into human consumption for nearly five years.'

There were a number of reasons for this decision. Since BST was a protein hormone it was digested enzymatically like any protein found in food. That was why cows had to be injected with BST for it to work. The FDA gave insulin as another example which had to be injected by diabetics to be effective – unless it was specially formulated to protect it from digestion. Further, BST was specific to cattle so if anybody was accidentally injected it would have no biological effect because it was not active in humans. Work in the 1950s had tried to treat human dwarfism in children by injecting them with bovine ST, but failed just because BST was not active in humans – a rare occasion where data already existed for human treatment with a new animal drug. Further, since cows produced BST naturally in their pituitary glands, treatment of cows with BST simply enhanced the amount that their bodies were already exposed to.

'Because cows naturally produce BST, it is already present in their milk. Thus, the milk we drink has always contained small quantities of BST. Treatment of cows with proposed low doses of BST does not significantly increase the concentrations of BST in milk. And, as stated above, BST in milk is digested if it is consumed, plus it is not active in humans. Also, the nutritive quality and manufacturing properties of milk from BST-treated cows are not altered.' The FDA added that BST produced by biotechnology was about 0.5% to 3% different in molecular structure from the BST naturally produced by the cow. The changes occurred at one of the 'tails' to the molecule and would make no difference to the lack of activity in humans.

Sponsors had to demonstrate that a new drug was effective and safe before it could be sold. Effectiveness meant that it did what the company claimed and had to be tested in multiple herds throughout the country under typical dairy management. Safety meant three things: safety of the food products to humans; safety to the target animals; and safety to the environment.

'We are aware of concerns that consumer confidence in milk and dairy products might be reduced if BST is approved' the FDA wrote. 'While your proposal to conduct market research on consumer acceptability of BST is an interesting and feasible idea, the Agency would alternatively recommend that strong efforts be made to educate consumers so that they clearly understand why milk from BST-treated cows is safe for consumption. Allowing emotional and unscientific arguments to rule the way food is produced or drugs are approved in this country would simply perpetuate a general lack of understanding about agriculture and science in general . . .

'As you know, by Federal law, social and economic need for a drug does not enter into FDA's approval decision. This would be a very difficult thing to predict with any drug. Generally, the laws are designed to make sure that a new drug is safe and effective, and then the marketplace determines whether it is economical and useful. Approval by FDA does not mean that a drug must be used, but rather that it can be used, if desired . . . Several aspects of the animal safety and efficacy work are yet to be completed, but as to consumption of milk from experimentally-treated cows, we have sufficient data to show that there is no harm to the consumer.'

These conclusions about safety have been repeated in

Europe. The European Commission arranged for a scientific seminar to study this subject and a summary of the conference was written by Frank Raymond, now retired from the UK Agricultural and Food Research Council, and Agner Niemann-Sorensen of the Danish National Institute of Animal Science.

They confirmed that it had been known since the 1930s that one of the main agents controlling growth and production in animals, including man, was a growth hormone, somatotropin, secreted by the pituitary gland. In general the activity of this hormone was species-specific so that, for example, BST secreted by the dairy cow, had no influence on human growth processes. It had also been shown with a number of animal species that injection of a pituitary extract from the same species would stimulate growth and milk production. This suggested that the rate of production might be limited by the amount of hormone being secreted.

'Effectively then, when somatotropin is injected into an animal it reinforces the natural production and actions of somatotropin . . . The present consensus is that BST-treated milk is nutritionally safe for human consumption'.

What about the cow? Safety includes her too. Raymond and Neimann-Sorensen quoted the UK Farm Animal Welfare Council who said in December 1987 that, while there was no evidence to date of any welfare problems, there were areas where additional scientific information was needed to allow a more considered opinion. Since then, further work has been done and Raymond's report says that data are now available from cows that are entering their fourth lactation treatment with BST, without any measurable clinical effects. Other studies have also shown that calves from BST-treated cows show no abnormal physical or physiological features; many heifer calves have been bred successfully and are now ready to enter milk production. It adds that concern about welfare, per se, mainly related to possible injury or distress resulting from the injection of BST. The replacement of daily by 2- or 4-weekly injections greatly reduced this risk. But a key point for decision remained whether, if BST treatment was permitted, injections should be made by vets rather than by the herdsman. This and other welfare matters still had to be resolved, and Raymond said that they were being addressed – for unless clear evidence could be provided that BST caused no harm to animal health or welfare, consumer resistance could lead to a fall in the demand for milk and dairy products which could more than outweigh any economic advantage resulting from the use of BST.

His summary was that 'the indications to date are that, provided it is properly used, BST will be given a clean "bill of health".'

Despite this consensus, a campaign against the use of BST has been waged. Its most vigorous supporter is the American Jeremy Rifkin, who is fighting to hold back biotechnology on many fronts. He is the charming, plausible and persuasive founder and president of the Washington-based lobby group, the Foundation on Economic Trends (FET). He has been particularly skilled in using American legal processes to challenge developments in genetic engineering but also uses standard campaigning techniques to stimulate direct action and wide media coverage. He argues that 'it is time for the federal government to construct a regulatory procedure that would provide a comprehensive foresight analysis for all decisions regarding the development and commercial application of genetic engineering technology. The environmental, economic, social, and cultural impacts of each new genetically engineered product or program must be scrutinised.'

Rifkin has linked up with a wide variety of groups from

consumer organisations to dairy farmers to form an anti-BST coalition; he has attempted to corral the supermarkets into joining this coalition; and he has drawn on scientists to question the safety of BST. In particular, he has found in Samuel Epstein a scientist who has criticised BST.

Epstein's claims about BST suggest its use could include premature growth stimulation in infants, breast growth in young children, and breast cancer in adult females. He also implies that stress effects from BST in cattle could lead to viral infections in them, and that the relationship between these viruses and the AIDS complex is of further concern. Further, he claims that the increased risk of infectious diseases noted in efficacy trials and presumably stress-induced is likely to result in increased antibiotic treatment and antibiotic levels in milk. He wants both the incidence of diseases and the levels of antibiotics to be monitored because of possible antibiotic resistance. And he says the effect of hormonal treatment is likely to mobilise carcinogens from body fat and increase their milk levels, a matter of particular concern in young infants.

Epstein's catalogue of catastrophes, with its references to sexual abnormalities and infections including cancer and AIDS, has been firmly challenged. In America, the FDA addressed these observations in letters to the editors of the papers concerned. To the *Los Angeles Times* it commented that Epstein's piece contained 'some factual information and a great deal of scientific exaggeration, designed more to frighten than enlighten . . . The exaggerations (e.g., that increased bacterial infections in cows will require treatment with antibiotics that will pass to man and create antibiotic-resistant infections in the general population, that somehow the use of bovine somatotropin may create infections in man similar to AIDS, that cows are widely contaminated with carcinogens in their body fat) do a significant disservice to your readers who do not have first hand knowledge of their lack of scientific merit.'

It is difficult for the layman to judge between scientists when they dispute the facts. But Epstein's reputation goes before him. In particular, he was the subject of detailed criticism by the British epidemiologist Richard Peto in an article in *Nature* in March 1980. Peto wrote: 'A particularly good example of the biased writings of politically active environmentalists is Samuel Epstein's *The Politics of Cancer* . . . written to inflame political passions against environmental carcinogens, . . . parts of it are well worth reading. However, the political punch is often achieved at the expense of scientific accuracy and balance . . . (It) is very useful as a source of reference to original papers, but it is not itself a reliable secondary reference because the material presented is so often distorted.'

Peto analysed particular examples of distortion and concluded, 'I found that in many places where he discussed data with which I was familiar inaccuracies were present, almost always in the direction of accentuating the need for battle with the devils of industry . . . Epstein . . . seems certain that the majority of human cancer is caused by chemical and physical agents in the environment and could be prevented by their testing and regulation. There is no sound scientific basis for this certainty . . . (He) seems certain that at least a quarter of all cancer deaths are attributable to occupational exposure to carcinogens. There is as yet no good evidence for hazards of anything like this magnitude, and there is clear evidence that many of his particular claims are exaggerated.'

But, if Peto is profoundly unimpressed by Epstein's science, he has more sympathy with his politics. He knows that the tobacco industry is just as guilty of distortion, and writes: 'My criticisms of Epstein's science, however, must be viewed in the light of the continued resistance of many industries to reasonable controls . . . For the moment, the "politics of cancer" is dominated on both sides by exaggeration.'

Indeed, Epstein willingly admits as much. He quotes Plutarch: 'He who in a time of factions takes neither side shall be disfranchised.' He is quite clear which faction he supports and why, and Peto shows he has been ready to exaggerate so that his criticisms are bound up with his clear commitment to his chosen faction. As with cancer, so with BST, dozens of scientists disagree with Epstein. Hundreds of scientific papers have pronounced BST safe. To the layman, it looks extremely unlikely that all are wrong and Epstein right. The only large unanswered question about safety is one which Epstein passes over. It concerns long-term risks. By definition, that question must remain unanswered until BST has been around for a long time. Even there, the trials on human dwarfism more than 30 years ago give a pointer which is seldom if ever available for a new product.

Raymond and Neimann-Sorensen say that BST is safe for humans and cows. What about for farmers? The advance of technology has driven tens of thousands of small farmers out of business, and BST may accelerate that process. The two authors ask about the likely form and scale on which the technique might be adopted; the probable economic and social consequences if it were adopted; and the acceptability of the technique to consumers and the wider society.

A brief historical break: when milk quotas came to Europe on April Fools' Day 1984, dairy farmers' incomes collapsed in the muddle. Today, they are back to or above where they were in the 1970s. Before quotas, the price of milk fell steadily, so the only way for farmers to maintain their incomes was to sell more milk. Quotas blocked off that route. The only way to maintain income was to produce milk more cheaply.

There are two ways to do that. You can use cheaper

feeds, above all grass; and you can become more efficient. For 50 years now increasing efficiency has had two strands, better management and better technology. Together they have seen cows becoming steadily more productive, milk steadily cheaper and dairy farmers steadily fewer. This history lies behind the fear that BST, which can increase a cow's milk output by 20%, could drive 20% of farmers out of business. It will not have anything like that effect. Various attempts have been made to forecast the impact of BST, and Raymond summarises them into six points.

The first is that BST is not a radical new discovery which will revolutionise milk production, but one of the continuing series of developments which have steadily improved the efficiency of milk production over the last 40 years. Second, it should only be adopted by the individual farmer if it allows him to produce a litre of milk more cheaply. This could limit the uptake of BST so that its overall effect on EEC milk production would be likely to be well below the 2.5% increase in milk output per cow recorded every year in the early 1980s. Third, adoption of BST could speed up the rate of decline in dairy cow numbers in the eight main milk-producing Member States by about 10%, with cow numbers falling by 5.4 million by 1995, compared with 4.9 million if BST is not used. Because routine treatment with BST would be more practicable on larger than smaller dairy farms, much of this additional fall in cow numbers would be on smaller farms. However, this would represent only a small increase in the present rate of loss of small farms. But Raymond's fourth point is that BST could be of particular economic value in helping small dairy farmers to adjust their milk output to quota and to take advantage of seasonal price differentials, and his fifth that such use of BST, if it led to more level output of milk, should improve the economy of milk processing factories. Finally, he summarises by saying that BST would only be used in situations in which it would reduce the cost of milk production, that this could limit the scale of uptake and so the effect on the price of milk. Overall, therefore, consumers should benefit – as they have from the many other technical advances that have been made in milk production.

This assessment of the commercial impact of BST is in line with others carried out at Wye College and by the Milk Marketing Board at Thames Ditton. It led the seminar convened by the European Commission to conclude that 'if the necessary health and welfare conditions are satisfied, the preferred course would appear to be for the use of BST to be authorised for milk production in the Community, but only under strictly controlled conditions'. Raymond and Niemann-Sorensen listed this set of possible conditions:

- only sustained-release preparations could be used, and daily injections would be prohibited
- manufacturers and suppliers of BST would only be permitted to sell to 'registered' dairy farms; to qualify for the register a farm must have obtained advice from a veterinary surgeon and a dairy nutritionist on the correct administration of BST and on changes needed in the feeding and management regime
- each registered farm would have prescribed veterinary visits to check on animal health and welfare
- dairy farmers would be actively advised to delay administration of BST until after the cow had conceived.

The seminar accepted that even such supervision could not completely prevent misuse of BST. But it considered that misuse under the proposed system would be small compared with what might happen if BST, readily available in other countries yet virtually undetectable in use, were banned.

The Commission has imposed a delay on a decision about BST. While it lasts, further studies will be completed. They cover consumer and farmer attitudes and the likely economic impact, and more work on the safety of BST-treated cows and the quality of their milk. Few doubt that, both in Europe and America, the licensing authorities will clear it on grounds of safety, efficacy and quality. In America, where licensing should be completed some time in 1990, the battle will then move to the market place. In Europe, attempts are being made to introduce a new criterion, the so-called fourth hurdle of social and economic need. That is where the debate will focus during the delay imposed by the Commission.

THE POLITICS OF NOVEL PROCESSES

Food irradiation and BST have become party political issues here and elsewhere, a fate which hinders assessment of the balance of risks and benefits which would come from their use. Labour MP's who admit privately that they have few worries about BST won't vote that way; Tory members who have reservations about irradiation will end up in the Yes lobby. Much of the argument is about how to police such new technologies, which has added another political dimension to the struggle.

The consequences for irradiation showed up in the House of Commons debate of 12 July 1989. Tories to a man (we may include Mrs Ann Winterton, who admitted that as a previous master of foxhounds nobody had called her mistress of anything, and addressed Miss Betty Boothroyd as Mister Deputy Speaker until instructed by Miss Boothroyd to call her Madam) supported irradiation. Labour to a man (no woman spoke from the opposition benches) opposed.

The government, in the person of Minister of Agriculture John MacGregor, took the broad approach. The World Health Organisation and the Food and Agriculture Organisation said that properly controlled irradiation of food was safe. So did the National Consumer Council. The European Commission planned to allow it in the Community and in harmony with this the government now proposed to license it, where appropriate, in the United Kingdom. Nobody – producer, manufacturer, retailer or consumer – need use it unless they chose to. All irradiated foods must be labelled, all applications must be approved before – and monitored when in – use, and all imports must be covered by similar controls.

The opposition targeted the nitty gritty. Dr David Clark said it was impossible to test whether food had been irradiated, much less re-irradiated. This made a nonsense of labelling. So, unless listed on menus as irradiated prawn curry or kilograyed chicken Chasseur, did the fact that most irradiated food would be used in catering. Mr Martyn Jones, after adding the British Medical Association and the Institute of Environmental Health Officers to those opposed, said that irradiation created small quantities of exotic chemicals such as peroxidated fatty acids and hydroxylated aromatics, Mr Frank Cook asked 'Do Ministers follow that?', Mr Jones thought not, and Mr Alan Williams brought both free radicals and hydroxylated benzine rings into this debate. He also reported his discovery that if he went through the irradiating machine it would kill him. He did not tell members what would happen if he was popped in an oven, sealed in a can, deep frozen, or even micro-waved.

In summary, the government was determined to see nothing but good in the process and believed that irradiation helped make food safe, while the opposition saw nothing but bad and warned that it could be used to pass off poor food as good. The adversarial habits of the House of Commons prevented any attempt to balance risks against benefits.

The Food Safety Bill proposes a full licensing system under central government control, plus comprehensive documentation and recording, with the aim of ensuring that customers know what they are getting, doses can be verified and irradiated foods traced. Existing controls on good manufacturing practices will be maintained and labelling is to be compulsory. Critics maintain that such controls cannot be adequate until a test for radiation is available and there remains a risk that irradiation will be used to clean up substandard food. Given the probable consumer response, however, it is unlikely that large amounts of irradiated food will rapidly reach the market.

BST also faces problems of control. Before it meets them, it may need to vault the fourth hurdle. Comnnoisseurs of bureaucoco will find much to enjoy in the debate.

The champion of the fourth hurdle is Ken Collins, MEP. He set out his views when he spoke in October 1989 to the annual conference of the National Office of Animal Health (NOAH) which is the trade association of the veterinary products industry. His central points were that product development cannot ignore its likely impact on society and that industry must recognise a responsibility far wider than science and its shareholders. He argued that this responsibility should be reflected in the licensing process by assessing the social and economic impact of new products, and should be as binding as assessments of safety, efficacy and quality. He added: 'Without developing something along the lines of a fourth hurdle, rest assured there will be a political struggle over every new growth or yield promoting pharmaceutical product that you develop.'

Put like that, few would disagree. But how do you do it? Walter Beswick, president of the British Veterinary Association (BVA), had previously written to Collins pointing out the difficulties. He asked what should be measured, and with what ruler?

The difficulty is best seen with hindsight. Suppose a fourth hurdle had existed at the dawn of the motor age. The party of the horse would have ridiculed the need for a novelty which would get stuck in mud, ruts and rivers, could scarcely climb hills, travel across country nor clear the smallest fence. What conceivable need was there to fill the roads with men waving red flags? Blacksmiths would have beaten rhythms of contempt on anvils up and down the country, backed by a chorus of feed merchants, wheelwrights, cart makers, ploughmen and stable hands. Copers would have grown hoarse in rejection, jockeys have split their silks and the cavalry would have jingled its spurs. The party of the motor, reluctant to admit the force of these objections, would have spoken for individual freedom. Mechanics would have praised the engine, garage hands the nuts and bolts, oilmen the wellhead, Ford the production line, Firestone the rubber tyre, and the youthful Nuvolari would have polished his new set of racing goggles. The coroner who spelt out to his court the lessons to be learnt from the first death of the motor age so that everyone could be sure it would also be the last, might be forgiven for failing to foresee motorway madness, and there were as yet no ecologists to raise fears about lead in petrol, acid rain or greenhouse gases. The personal mobility which has been the transforming effect of the motor age on the twentieth century would almost certainly have gone unremarked. So would the immobility of traffic jams.

The hurdle to cope with that debate would have been one of sturdy construction. Even now, economists are bad and social psychologists worse at forecasting and measuring our needs. Imagine however they enjoyed today's skills and ask if they could have forecast and measured the social and economic need for the motor age. Then ask, if the difficulties were insuperable in 1900 do they remain so in 1990 for a product like BST?

Beswick and the BVA thought that they did, for they quickly ran up against the problems of identifying what was to be measured, let alone measuring it. Should it be that no one's income should suffer, or no jobs should be lost, or there should be no change in farm size or regional distribution of production? It was possible to define numerous indices of the social and economic effects of technological change, but agreeing thresholds of acceptable rates of change would be extremely difficult and proving a new technology would cause changes which were likely to exceed the acceptable levels would be impossible.

Beswick agreed with Collins that the heart of the matter was consumer concerns and influence on decisions. He suggested that the market was where consumers decided the fate of new products and that it would work better with much less secrecy, much more labelling, assured enforcement of the rules, and more quality schemes. But Collins was unimpressed. He told NOAH 'it is surely correct that society, collectively, should make judgments about the desirability of the clearly far-reaching consequences which may follow from the application of some technologies . . .

'Your companies can continue to oppose the concept of a fourth hurdle for growth promoting veterinary medicine. You can continue to make the assertion that the market should choose and you can continue to ignore your responsibilities to the society which in the end consumes the product of the technologies which you employ . . . On the other hand your companies can . . . work with legislators to develop procedures and authorisation systems which take into acount the legitimate concern of consumers while giving a central place to science. You can demonstrate that you take seriously the claims your industry sometimes makes about its responsibilities for the society around you . . .

'My objective is to create a licensing system which is rational and objective but also capable of accommodating and expressing the worries, and expectations, of those I am elected to represent.' What he did not say was how it could be done.

There are various methods, applied for example to the design of large new chemical plants, which help designers think through a wide range of outcomes. These methods ask a series of 'what-if?' questions as an aid to clear, comprehensive thinking about what might happen and above all what might go wrong. They aim, so far as possible, to expose the otherwise unforeseen and could be adapted to help similar clarity of thinking about new pharmaceuticals. But they cannot resolve the question of need. That question is a value judgment – a jargon phrase meaning choice. All choices about the future entail guesswork and this makes the design of a fourth hurdle extremely susceptible to logical rickets. That is why the outcome has been left to the marketplace.

Collins points out the difficulty of this with BST. Because there is no detectable difference in milk from BST-treated cows it cannot be labelled to allow consumer choice. There is no such thing as BST-free milk so it is impossible to identify, much less label, milk produced with or without injected BST.

The growth of organic food production and the arrival of the organic register and label offers – or will offer – a way out of this. Here is organically-grown milk at one price; here conventionally-grown milk at another. Consumers could choose and the market would decide – though the small amounts of organically-grown milk at present available would limit the speed at which that choice could spread.

Collins is a tough, wily and imaginative politician who

may find a way to avoid a logically-ricketty fourth hurdle. He is entirely right to say that companies making pharmaceutical – or any other – products want to work with the minimum of uncertainty; commerce is the first to accept it needs to know where it stands. He is similarly accurate about consumers. What he has not yet made clear is why the fourth hurdle should not remain the marketplace. There is also a clear likelihood that a ricketty fourth hurdle will revive the trans-Atlantic trade war already rumbling over hormones and if it does the clashes over beef will echo as no more than a distant wheeze.

It is widely accepted by scientists that the two technologies, food irradiation now quite old and BST well-known for decades but newly available in use, are safe with responsible use. Both have been caught up in political battles which have aroused consumer fears but which in the end are far less about safety than about control – specifically, who is to control the responsible use of individual processes with important social and economic consequences? This issue also dominates the debate about genetic engineering.

The European Parliament, given its views on growth promoting hormones in beef, has been a focus of resistance to the spread of these technologies. Although the EEC will probably accept limited use of food irradiation by the end of 1990, and of BST sometime after that, the political outcome will remain uncertain until the final decisions are made.

CHAPTER SEVEN:
The Biotechnical Future

Biotechnology hits human health and welfare everywhere. With the possible exception of medicine, food and farming are the largest targets.

The central, and most sensitive, zone of biotechnology is genetic manipulation. This is biological *Lego.*® The pieces are the genes which control such basic processes as reproduction, growth, lactation and health. We know just how to click them neatly together once we've found them, but at present the box of pieces is almost empty. That means there is a limit, rapidly reached, to how many new models can be made and the major task is to find a lot more pieces.

Genetic Lego comes in a number of sets, among them those for plants and mammals, and you can use and re-use the pieces to make completely different models. But there are formidable difficulties: for example, the mammals' set when full would hold 100,000 pieces and at the moment has around 1,500 in it. These pieces can be clicked into cows or sheep or mice, while the plant pieces can move just as readily from trees to grasses to brassicas. Quite a lot of the pieces can be used in both sets at the same time, and the same is true for other sets covering birds or bacteria, reptiles or insects.

Human genes fit easily into the mammals' set. It seems that once nature hits on a method – say, for making milk in mammals – it sticks to it. The machinery for making milk is very similar indeed in us, in cows and in sheep, and in duck-billed platypuses. This sort of similarity keeps popping up. For example the gene which controls cell division in yeast has been found in humans where it is also involved in controlling cell division.

The implications of these possibilities are immense and the debate about their use correspondingly intense. Dr Roger Straughan of Reading University was commissioned by the National Consumer Council (NCC) to spell them out in detail. He wrote that 'applications of genetic manipulation to agriculture are basically intended to enhance the useful and desirable characteristics of plants, animals and microbes and to eliminate the undesirable ones. The overall aim is, therefore, to improve the quality and to increase the quantity and profitability of food products.' He quotes Miksche and Clarke: 'Biotechnology research offers a major opportunity to tailor food products to public demands. Existing crop and animal products can be modified through genetic engineering; new crops and new products can be developed.'

Nobody doubts that the possibilities exist. The BST debate shows how different people react. What are the arguments for and against?

Probably the strongest reason for backing biotechnological Lego is this:

What would the world be once bereft
Of wet and wildness? Let them be left
O let them be left, wildness and wet;
Long live the weeds and the wilderness yet.

The expansion in food supplies up to the nineteenth century came from taking more land into production. The expansion of supplies in the second half of the twentieth century has come from increasing the output of that acreage so that now in developed countries land once used for farming is surplus to requirements and is being taken out of agriculture – although this welcome development has been achieved at the cost of some unsatisfactory side effects.

As the world's population increases, we seem to have little choice but to keep up the increases in production while striving to keep down the side effects. One of these is that Gerard Manley Hopkins' weeds, wilderness and wet are disappearing. The best-known case is the tropical rain forests but there are sharp political arguments about Antarctica as well as about millions of Hopkins' pockets dotted from pole to pole. The more land we use for food and farming, the more devastation of Amazon and Antarctica, and the fewer of Hopkins' pockets. This threat will double over the next 40 years as the human population doubles. It is what James Lovelock was referring to when he said provokingly that all food should be synthesised by industry. Biotechnology could be a very powerful contributor to this process.

Thus backing for biotechnology comes from the urgent need to do less damage to our environment. This is now a fundamental imperative. As Mark Cantley, one of the Brussels' bureaucrats responsible, puts it, the goal is the beneficial application of biotechnology to the maintenance and improvement of health and well-being, local environments and the global ecosystem. He argues that to sustain such a growing population in civilised conditions without destroying the planet's continuing ability to support human and other life, will call for all the intelligence and understanding which we possess concerning the management of living systems.

An equally strong argument is that genetic manipulation techniques are excellently suited to solving many of the immense difficulties of tropical and semi-tropical agriculture. They could complete the job of the green revolution, and solve all problems of food shortage. At the very least, we can now choose between producing less from more by maintaining traditional methods of food production (or even by spreading them more widely over the land in parts of the world like Europe and America where large acreages of disused farmland are now available) or more from less as we have increasingly been learning to do over the last 50 years. So we should recite Hopkins before we start to think, and then we should think unusually hard about throwing out sensible ways of producing more from less.

But, if backing for biotechnology comes from the urgent need to do less damage to our environment, so does backing away from it. The fears are many. The first is of the dangers coiled in the unknown, especially that we may create organisms which will return to plague us. Another is of desecration, that tampering with DNA will leave the sacred in tatters. Another is of irresponsibility, that we lack the wisdom to control a new generation of genies let out of the bottle of science. Another again is the fear that industrial control of biotechnology will jam the whole world into a commercial headlock, so ending traditional farming practices and the crops, animals and lifestyles which go with them.

There are grounds for all those fears. Most of them diminish if we can be certain of our ability to control biotechnology, a subject now of profound concern to politically-motivated groups throughout the developed world. There are strong grounds also for the fear that the greatest risk is to do nothing, since biotechnology can help to feed tomorrow's world on less land than we use today, convert wastes into unpolluting or even useful products, increase energy efficiency, boost the use of renewable raw materials in tomorrow's industry and help to restore the scars and wounds of centuries of exploitation.

But, says reaction, we are overfed and overstocked.

And, adds masochism, with frills, fats and fancy goods. Further, says vegetarianism, we brutalise the beasts and so ourselves. And, chimes in holism, we split nature as we split the atom. Eat right, grow less, store less.

Cantley and others argue that biotechnology must contribute to this process. 'Interest groups seriously concerned with the maintenance and restoration or enhancement of the environment, of ecosystems, should recognise the potential of recent advances in biotechnology for enabling their objectives to be achieved.'

It clarifies the argument to distinguish, with Straughan, between the safety of a process and the safety of a product. For example, the processes of wind or water turbines, coal or nuclear power, make the product electricity; each of these processes can be more or less dangerous, as can the final product of electricity depending how we control its use. Even then however there are difficulties. Thus on the safety of the processes of genetic manipulation, Straughan asks: 'Why cannot the apparently straightforward question, is it safe? be given a straightforward yes or no answer? This is because the question in fact conceals considerable complexities, which arise from the following factors.

'Scientists cannot "prove" by empirical investigations that one experiment or class of experiments is more hazardous than another without undertaking experiments which are in fact hazardous. Scientist cannot "prove" by tests and experiments that a particular event will never happen in the future. We can talk only in terms of apparent probabilities. Factual evidence provided by experts cannot, therefore, conclusively answer the question, is it safe? Decisions about risk and safety will inevitably involve value judgments.

'Making decisions about the safety of genetic manipulation processes, therefore, requires that somewhere the balance has to be struck between the paralysis of extreme caution and the irresponsibility of uncontrolled experimentation. The striking of this balance means making value judgments about complex social/ethical issues for which there are no simple answers.' Thus when we grow food more efficiently we benefit because it costs less and the environment gains because farming takes up less room; both of these mean pressure on small farmers who are forced out of business, though neither alters the fact that small farmers have suffered in this way since farm productivity started to rise 250 years ago.

Recently, an extensive review of these issues appeared in the Royal Commission on Environmental Pollution's report on *The Release of Genetically Engineered Organisms to the Environment*, published in July 1989. What follows is a summary.

Until the beginning of 1988 there had been, worldwide, about 30 deliberate releases of genetically engineered organisms (GEOs). In 1988 there was a dramatic increase in the number of experimental trials involving plants, and by the end of the year about 80 experimental releases had taken place. Six of these were in the UK. Some products, such as vaccines and other pharmaceuticals, are already on the market, having satisfied strict safety tests.

GEOs released into the environment could produce noticeable changes in the countryside, could have an economic impact, could pose a threat to human health and could conceivably affect major environmental processes such as weather patterns, the nitrogen cycle or other regenerative soil processes. The report gives the following examples.

Ice-minus bacteria are GEOs designed to compete with microbes which induce ice formation, and so to reduce frost damage to plants like strawberries; their action might also lead to changes in local climate by preventing the formation of rain droplets. The US Office of Technology Assessment (OTA) concluded after two studies that the likelihood of climatic change was negligible even if ice-minus bacteria had large-scale agricultural use.

Rhizobium bacteria can be altered to improve nitrogen fixation in soils. Again the OTA concluded that the chance of adverse effects on the nitrogen cycle was very remote, and that normal crop rotation could produce greater changes than microbial innoculations to the patterns of nitrogen distribution and movement in an ecosystem.

GEOs can be inserted into plants to confer resistance to attack by insects; might the insect-repelling chemical which they produce end up in parts of the plant eaten by animals or humans? If so, would we be able to make them safe to eat as we already do with plants like rhubarb, potatoes and certain beans?

The Royal Commission next considered information on how foreign organisms establish themselves in a new environment. It began by looking at natural communities which are in general resistant to invasion by alien species. Gardens in Britain contain many thousands of species and varieties of non-native plants but few of them escape and establish themselves in the wider countryside. When they do, however, problems can arise. An example is the way rhododendrons have become a weed which has colonised large areas of the countryside.

One analysis has looked at 1,058 documented invasions of alien plants, animals or micro-organisms into the British Isles. About one in ten became established, and of these about one in ten became pests (ie, about ten out of the original 1,058), varying in severity from relatively minor to highly damaging. But since most failed invasions go unrecorded, the probability of an invader becoming established is much less than these figures suggest – and none was screened for safety prior to arrival.

The report said that the diversity of habitats which existed in nature was an important factor contributing to the resilience of the environment in relation to micro-organisms. A micro-organism can colonise only a few of these niches, for a typical handful of soil contains a large number of micro-organisms (as many as ten billion in each gram) with a wide range of differing nutritional requirements, preferred temperatures for growth, abilities to tolerate acidity, needs for oxygen and other characteristics. It is therefore inherently unlikely that a micro-organism could be engineered which would dominate more than a small proportion of the wide range of habitats to which it would have access.

'We conclude that, although the environment is generally resilient, resistant to invasion by alien organisms and robust to biological perturbations, it is probable that some organisms, once released to the environment, will become established. Most are likely to pose no hazard but others may cause varying degrees of disturbance which, in the extreme, could have serious environmental consequences.'

Which ones? As we have seen, prediction of environmental impacts is difficult and the science underpinning it not well developed. It is extremely difficult to determine why one species becomes a pest while one or more of its close relatives fails to do so.

But ability to predict the outcome of a release is likely to be greater if the GEO is a modified version of an organism common in the locality of the release; its behaviour in the environment is well-known; the genetic modification is limited in scope; the proper ties of the new genetic material and its interaction with the original organism are well understood; and the quantities to be released are not excessive.

GEOs in plants could be spread by pollen to other plants with undesirable consequences. Most inserted genes are likely to be ones which already exist in nature, so release of the GEOs may produce only a slight increase in the number of such genes already potentially available for transfer. But any GEO should be assumed to be capable of spreading widely, and that assumption then convincingly challenged. The Commission points out that this will mean working out how genes spread from a GEO could be recovered and eradicated.

The European Parliament has recently adopted a report which among other things calls for a moratorium, and consideration of a total ban, on the release of genetically engineered organisms. But the Royal Commission says: 'We do not consider that there should be a ban or moratorium on releases either in general or for specific categories. If our recommendations for controlling the release of GEOs are implemented, we consider that it should be possible to identify cases that raise concerns and deal with them appropriately on an individual basis, if necessary preventing them from taking place.' Each case needs to be scrutinised by a national committee of experts (the Release Committee).

The Release Committee would tabulate procedures to minimise risk. Fundamentally, this would pursue a step-by-step approach. Thus initial trials would be fully-contained in a laboratory. This would tell us little about how far gene transfer mechanisms observed in the laboratory might operate in nature. Creating enclosed artificial environments (or microcosms, for example by bringing a lake into a large greenhouse) offers a stage between laboratory testing and field trials. While only a partial aid, because of obvious difficulties about the accuracy of such artificial results in a natural setting, properly-used microcosms would be helpful predictive tools.

Other aspects of the step-by-step approach also help make sure that changes do not lead to dangerous uncertainties. For example, when planning to introduce an engineered virus: first, change the natural virus only by putting in a marker so that the spread can be monitored;

then add genes weakening the virus so that it survives less well and again monitor spread; test and monitor whether these changes alter the working of the virus, especially its ability to express proteins; finally, add the gene designed to increase the effectiveness of the virus. Various weakening or crippling genes might be added. For example, there is a gene known as HOK which, suitably enough, releases an electric shock. This, when Legoed into a bacteria, kills it. It can be clicked in with another gene which stops the shock from happening immediately.

The ability to recover and clean-up an organism, at least during trial stages, would be helpful. Since clean-up is often likely to be impossible after commercial release, the Royal Commission says it would be prudent to work on the assumption that, once released, it may not be possible totally to eradicate an organism from the environment. As well, close monitoring both during and after any release is essential to identify any changes, as is the international exchange of information thus acquired to make sure that any unexpected problems become rapidly known to both workers and the public.

The Royal Commission says that statutory control of GEOs must be put in place which incorporate the above provisions and build on existing controls in the Health and Safety at Work Act. Licences for release, and for each stage of any planned release, should be issued by the Secretary of State for the Environment and the Health and Safety Commission (HSC), acting jointly. They would be advised by the Release Committee. The report goes on to say that 'the potential benefits which we foresee are likely to arise from exploitation of genetic engineering could be frustrated by public opposition motivated by fear of the unknown. Relevant information relating to a proposed release of genetically engineered organisms to the environment should therefore be made available to the public before the release takes place. Further, this information must be open to examination and assessment by suitably qualified scientists and others who may be engaged by public interest bodies for the purpose. A field trial, as well as the sale or supply of a product, may give rise to concern, so there must be public access to information at several stages of development . . .

'The arrangements we recommend represent a significantly greater degree of public access to information than is the case for pharmaceuticals and other products. We consider them to be justified by the likely high level of public interest in, and concern about, the release of genetically engineered organisms.'

These conclusions are broadly echoed by American experience. Thus Bernard Dixon writing in *The Guardian* accepted that ecologists, whose expert knowledge of the biosphere might be expected to make them oppose the dissemination of transgenic organisms, have expressed confidence that they can be handled safely, and quotes 'the Ecological Society of America, who: "support the timely development of environmentally sound products, such as improved agricultural varieties, fertilisers, pest control agents, and micro-organisms for waste treatment, through the use of advanced biotechnology within the context of a scientifically-based regulatory policy that encourages innovation without compromising sound environmental management".'

Dixon underlines the Royal Commission's acceptance of the importance of public concern. 'The recently established UK Genetics Forum has asked the Royal Commission to recommend a partial moratorium . . . During that period, engineered organisms would be released only for purposes of furthering our understanding of their behaviour in natural ecosystems. This would be a reasonable strategy, allowing time for the knowledge base to be extended before definitive applications are contemplated in the course of time.

'Unless public and political confidence is fostered by such prudence, the outcome (here and in other parts of Europe too) could well be success for those who are calling for a total ban on controlled release. And the certain results of that strategy are an end to learning, stagnation for the knowledge base – and the feckless aborting of a potentially beneficent technology.'

The changes brought by biotechnology can sustain two of three thrusts which will increasingly dominate food production and consumption. More fresh foods will be eaten; more lightly-processed 'as fresh' foods will be eaten; more highly-specialised processed foods will be eaten – ranging from what the Japanese call function foods (like the oats which reduce cholesterol) to high nutrient density or other designer foods.

The first will include more organic or non-chemical produce which, at present tiny, will grow rapidly. Of total British food sales of £33 billion, organic foods in 1989 were less than £50 million, or not much over 0.1%. As they grow in volume, they will shrink in price. Safeways intends to get the price for organic foods down from premiums of 20% to 150% to somewhere nearer 10%. Some sectors will grow faster than others. Organic meat, says Safeways, will never be a major competitor to conventional meat. To expand the market 'the crusading approach must be taken out of organic meat. It must become a strictly commercial venture.' And the price must fall sharply: 'Already a very small sector are buying organic meat at anything up to double the price of conventional meat, but it must be said that the majority of these consumers have incomes to match their principles.'

The second will see some of the new technical developments described above as well as changes in agricultural practice as growers use more refined methods to produce and protect their crops. Better disease forecasting and integrated pest management, greater inbred disease resistance, and environmentally-sensitive crop protection techniques will all see farm chemical use falling slowly.

The last could see yet another agricultural revolution as crops are broken down into components, perhaps at rural refineries, and recombined into products meeting both pleasurable and nutritional criteria at a range of prices. In this, the food industry will match other areas of manufacturing. A recent report from the Department of Trade and Industry (DTI) says that all manufacturing in this country is belatedly abandoning low-cost, high-volume standardised production for stable markets in favour of flexible computer-controlled batch production of demand-led, technically sophisticated products for rapidly changing international consumer markets.

The DTI tells us that manufacturers will design and assemble components bought from global suppliers into products sold internationally in a new knowledge-based competitive environment. The domination of price in the 1950s and 1960s and of quality in the 1970s are now giving way to demands for highly personalised and specialised goods.

Just as food lent itself convincingly to now outmoded mass production techniques so it lends itself equally to these wider industrial trends of subtlety, sophistication and personalised demands. As David Goodman, Bernardo Sorj and John Wilkinson put it in their book *From Farming to Biotechnology*: 'Once the basic biological requirements of subsistence are met, the "natural" content of food paradoxically becomes an obstacle to consumption. If increased intake is to be promoted while also observing current dietary recommendations, then food must be more highly processed to reduce the content of calories, unsaturated fats and sugars. Livestock and dairy products . . . are among the foods most threatened by these trends, as declining per capita beef consumption in the United States readily indicates. Conversely, industrial

147

techniques of "animal" protein production can be easily adapted to meet these dietary requirements; given their capacity to convert low-value carbohydrates into high-value proteins, these direct industrial methods will accelerate the transition from crop to biomass production in agriculture.'

The regulation of this evolving biotechnology will remain an extremely active area of debate with major ethical, legal and political implications – which once again makes it impossible to predict the outcome of the current round of legislation in Brussels, Westminster and elsewhere in Europe except to say it will be no more than the start of massive future law-making. The most persuasive approach would be to license products and processes one-by-one, following the sort of extensive and open assessments proposed by the Royal Commission. Probably, that is the approach which Europe will eventually take.

CHAPTER EIGHT :

The Interaction of Nutrition Policy with Nutrition Science

Arguments about what we eat in the end revolve around nutrition science. Because food is so politically sensitive, nutrition science is jostled by nutrition policy. That is split into two camps. Some of the muddle about diet comes from conflict between them.

One camp argues for a balanced and varied diet to give sufficient proteins, carbohydrates and fats plus adequate amounts of the essential nutrients such as amino acids and fatty acids as well as minerals and vitamins. The other camp argues that modern diet causes extensive health problems and wants a return to natural whole foods and an end to refined carbohydrates like white sugar and flour. The first, conservative, camp wants educated and informed consumers to choose for themselves what to eat. The second, radical, camp wants governments actively to discourage the sale of refined or fatty foods and to promote fresh whole foods. Thus, the politics of nutrition dovetail with the politics of free choice or greater centralised control.

A clear statement of the conservative view came when David Maclean, Parliamentary Secretary at the MAFF, addressed the Leatherhead Research Association symposium on food law in November 1989. He said: 'Quality is a subjective judgment with each consumer making his or her own decisions on the factors that make up quality. On that basis there can be no justification for the judgments of one group to be imposed from the centre on all consumers. It is the firm view of this government that so long as food is safe, hygienically produced and handled and is informatively labelled, as well as being available in adequate quantities at affordable prices, quality choice is a matter for the individual . . .'

Equally clear is the statement in the World Health Organisations' (WHO) book *Healthy Nutrition*. Author Professor Philip James writes: 'Many members of the public, and even people in nutrition education, view the balanced diet simply as a choice of foods needed to avoid vitamin, protein or mineral deficiencies. These are no longer the major nutrition problems in Europe, however; other diseases in which nutrition is an important component have developed despite the widespread use of the balance concept in nutrition education. With WHO and national committees now advocating a change in the diet of people in many European countries, perhaps a new approach is needed that avoids the implications of the balanced diet in the usual sense.'

To non-nutritionists, there is no obvious reason why the overlap between these camps should not be large and certainly many good reasons why it should be enlarged to shrink the muddle in the middle. Luckily, it is getting larger, but the growth is slowed because there are four active volcanoes in the landscape.

The first two are bigger than diet. One is the environment, pushed sharply up the agenda by Rachel Carson's *Silent Spring* in 1963 and rising ever since to reach the top with the greenhouse effect. Farming has been a hot topic in the environmental debate from the start, but food is now deeply involved as well whether through beef in the Amazon rain forest, shellfish in polluted coastal waters – or methane from livestock. According to James Lovelock, 'methane . . . is probably the most dangerous substance that we are injecting into the atmosphere. Methane is not only a key agent in the ozone hole phenomenon, but, much more seriously, it is a greenhouse gas that before long may overtake carbon dioxide in significance . . . Carbon dioxide can be cut back, if we have the will, but to stop the excessive release of methane gas from rice paddies and from cattle is all but impossible. For this reason even if the chlorofluorocarbons are banned altogether I do not expect the ozone hole to go away; it may even increase as more methane is added to the air.'

The Environmental Protection Agency (EPA) in America backs this diagnosis. It says that a 50% reduction in methane from grazing animals would contribute between half and three-quarters of the reduction needed to hold levels of methane in the atmosphere steady – or in short that ruminant livestock are more than half the problem with that particular greenhouse gas. But how do you work the trick?

Some will argue that we must eat less meat. Others will just as certainly say that our meat production must be as efficient as possible to minimise methane output. The EPA suggests that adding cottonseed oil to ruminant diets would help reduce methane output; or it may be that altering the rumen bacteria, perhaps by genetic engineering, would help. A study funded by the Dutch government, which warned that any rise in temperature faster than 0.1°C each ten years could lead to forest breakdown, suggested actively replacing some beef farming with forestry.

Whatever combination of these is used, ruminant numbers must be minimised. That gives one answer to the questions, who needs hormones or BST and its family of growth promoters or any other new technologies in efficient livestock production? Gaia – the environment – needs them. Similarly, some might argue for cutting rice production. Others will point out that high-yielding rice varieties and ultra-efficient storage will demand the use of the best modern technology, including pesticides or genetic engineering, to help minimise methane production. With any of these possibilities, politics enters a debate of increasingly evangelical intensity and food is in the middle.

The second volcano is consumerism, launched in this country by the Consumers' Association in 1957, pushed up the agenda two years after *Silent Spring* by Ralph Nader's *Unsafe At Any Speed* and also rising rapidly until placed very near the top not only by many western politicians but also by Mikhail Gorbachev. One result is that consumers now demand similar qualities – of continuity, reliability, value-for-money and safety – from food as from other goods despite the very different innate characteristics, production patterns and shelf-lives of cook-chill prawns and a Walkman. This overlaps with the third volcano, supply and demand.

From 1939 to the end of rationing in 1954, food in Britain was supply led. It stayed that way until beef and butter mountains lifted and wine and olive oil lakes deepened throughout Europe – features which saw the old battles for food supply give way to the new priorities of food demand. That finally put food alongside white, brown and all the other goods where the customer was already right. Food demand – giving consumers more of what they want – is now a priority in Russia and the Eastern Bloc as much as here. But when it comes to food and health, demand-led diets in developed countries are criticised by radical nutritionists who want governments actively to influence supply by incentives or laws which positively support quality. Inevitably, this keeps up the political temperature of food.

The fourth is ignorance. The volcano of basic nutrition science looked spent for decades. In 1959 there were five nutrition laboratories which a young British scientist could join. Three were in this country, one in Uganda and one in Jamaica. That was at the end of a 50-year golden age of nutritional science which saw the discovery of the vitamins, amino acids, essential fatty acids and other components of our food. By 1973 there was only one British base, the Dunn Nutrition Laboratory in Cambridge which itself was lucky to survive. The same is true in the rest of Europe and in America; throughout the world nutrition science had been allowed to slide. Although the Dunn today remains a world leader it operates with smaller funds than it did in 1973. There are more university departments studying food science than nutrition science, and the only break with that trend of neglect comes from the Agriculture and Food Research Council (AFRC) which is spending more on nutrition in the Institute of Food Research (IFR).

The director of the Dunn, Dr Roger Whitehead, admits that nutrition science lags way behind other biological sciences in the academic stakes, which makes it very difficult to catch the best brains. The subject is 'not always seen as important by the medical profession or branches of the food industry, and the way-out observations in the media confirm to these people how soft the science of nutrition can be.'

There are several reasons. Chief is that, after wartime food rationing, we thought we knew it all. A lot of money was spent on animal nutrition – to avoid the threat of ever being starved by war again – so that now we know far more about the science of feeding pigs or cows than of feeding you and me. Also, nutrition research is difficult. Tens of thousands of feeding experiments with laboratory animals were needed to work out the vitamins' story; and to be scientifically confident about human nutrition a similar number and more would be needed on us. They have not been done and it won't be easy, or in some cases possible, to do them. Nevertheless, the dormant nutrition volcano burst into life under the stimulus of work in Africa where doctors started thinking about diffe rences in disease patterns.

In 1966 the book *Diabetes, Coronary Thrombosis and the Saccharin Disease*, by T. L. Cleave, G. D. Campbell and N. S. Painter, was published. It has been decribed as a landmark in nutritional thinking. By then, Cleave had been a fibrc fan for at least 30 years – in 1936 he had been feeding protesting naval recruits on high-fibre diets. The ideas went back at least to the work of Sir Robert McCarrison in India 50 years earlier, and in fact had been known for centuries. McCarrison stressed the need for 'roughage' and criticised the western diet of white flour, sugar, jam and margarine, which he said caused disease.

Cleave's book stimulated both Hugh Trowell and Denis Burkitt to back the idea that the fibre found in traditional diets was responsible for the absence of coronary heart disease, diabetes, various bowel diseases and obesity in African patients, while its removal caused those afflictions in people eating over-refined foods. This challenge to modern food was the catalyst which revived interest in the science of nutrition. It got consumers going too: by 1982 the best-selling book in the United Kingdom was Eyton's *F-Plan Diet* advocating wholemeal cereals with ample vegetables and fruit.

Cleave, Trowell, Burkitt and their allies met many critics. Some felt that the evidence was inadequate or wrong, some that much more work was needed, some that part of the diet which was undigested could hardly have such profound effects, some that other aspects of the diet or other factors like exercise or alcohol were at work. But for 20 years the fibre argument has stood, and is now widely accepted by most nutritionists. Indeed, state-of-the-art nutrition science has gone beyond dietary fibre to the subtler notion of complex carbohydrates. Dr Ian Johnson of the IFR in Norwich says, punning intentionally or otherwise, that the dietary fibre approach is 'much in need of refinement . . . (it) covers a host of polysaccharides with different physico-chemical properties and biological effects.

'Recent research has revealed previously unknown physiological effects of the various components of dietary fibre. Furthermore, the properties of starch have been shown to be much more complex than previously suspected. Paradoxically, we now know that some components of dietary fibre are entirely broken down and assimilated in the gut, whereas a small proportion of starch in foods can survive digestion entirely . . . As a result . . . advice to consumers should be given in terms of foods rather than total fibre intake.'

Johnson himself is looking at the starch, gum and bran in oats which 'illustrate an important practical case of a complex carbohydrate food with a potentially favourable effect on human cholesterol metabolism . . . Oats are a rich source of viscous polysaccharides that modify the intestinal absorption of nutrients (and) provide a substantial quantity of readily fermentable carbohydrate in the colon.' But, while Johnson knows that a given amount of oat bran a day reduces cholesterol levels, including the low density cholesterol considered most damaging, he does not know why. It is probably because the bran inhibits cholesterol absorption in the gut; but it also ferments there and is absorbed into the bloodstream where it has additional physiological effects.

A further twist to this saga comes from the argument that it is not cholesterol but what happens to it which does the damage. Work at Philip James's Rowett Research Institute outside Aberdeen has looked at free radicals.

These highly-reactive molecules are bloodstream burglars which break and enter other molecules to get what they want, leaving disorder behind them. Fat cells leave chaos when burgled by free radicals; the breakdown products of cholesterol clog up the bloodstream, threatening coronary heart disease.

But free radicals are scavenged by vitamins C and E, which act as a police force against them. Eating more of these vitamins, whether in fresh fruit and vegetables or as synthetic supplements, may lessen the risk of heart attack. Work is continuing at the Rowett to assess this approach, which could join hands with oats to offer further protection against cholesterol and heart disease.

We, the consumers, are thus watching the debate unfold in front of us. Like much science as it develops, it is uncertain and messy. Arguments clash, hypotheses conflict, experiments confront and contradict – and the debate is not concealed in equations. It is in language we can understand about something which concerns us intimately. It is not surprising that interest groups and the media join the chase, and inevitable that they simplify.

The volcano of nutrition science retains an active core which continues to spew out debate. That fosters political disagreement. Hence David Maclean, in the speech already quoted above: 'If we are to adopt a policy of quality through choice our primary concern must be that the consumer is not confused or misled. He or she must be able to distinguish from the information on the label between foodstuffs which look alike but which are not the same and also those foodstuffs which are not what they appear to be. Better labelling laws can achieve this without resort to detailed standards . . . so as to provide the information which the consumer needs to know at the time of purchase . . .'

And hence Philip James in the book already quoted: 'The introduction of a greater variety of foods is unlikely to help alter disease patterns if the different foods remain consistently high in fat, saturated fatty acids, sugar or salt. The present need is to alter the proportion of food items consumed and to introduce new food products with a high nutrient density while continuing to encourage the consumption of many different types of food.'

Food is thus deeply embroiled in two arguments, one about the science of nutrition and one about whether markets are the most efficient way to meet our needs. Many food scares and single-issue campaigns are therefore also arguments between conservatives who believe the market should decide and radicals who believe it will distort. The battle is being fought with special vigour in a period which has seen a decline in the political regulation of much commercial activity, with consequences which have affected the quality of food.

CONSUMER GROUPS AND MEDIA INFLUENCE

Food policy is controlled by the government through its advisory committees. It is influenced by a vast number of groups which can be arranged in a three-way split between policy study organisations, industry, and consumers.

Policy study organisations, for example the Adam Smith Institute, the Centre for Policy Studies, or the Policy Studies Institute try to influence government directly by research linked to lobbying in support of their proposals. Where they are more interested in politics than pure research they will happily exploit issues for their political mileage. They focus on economic and social debate and argue for changes which they claim would better everybody's lot.

Success for such groups depends on their formal and informal contacts with policy makers, and on how persuasively they can influence the way ministers think. Food policy will be affected by the outcome. Thus the Adam Smith Institute has for the time being managed to move much economic and social policy towards deregulation, while the Centre for Policy Studies wants to put an end to the quasi-monopoly of the Milk and other Marketing Boards. The debate about food safety has inevitably been influenced by this climate, with growing demands from consumers that this is an area where stricter regulation is essential.

Industry groups are mainly the federations and associations which represent different sectors. They include the Food and Drink Federation (FDF), and related bodies like the Bacon and Meat Manufacturers Association, the Biscuit, Cake, Chocolate and Confectionery Alliance, or the Dairy Trades Federation. They embrace the Milk Marketing Boards, the National Farmers' Unions and the British Veterinary Association. They concern Environmental Health, and Trading Standards, Officers, and other Trades' Union groups like the Transport and General Workers Union which now houses what used to be the National Union of Agricultural and Allied Workers. They cover the Fertiliser Manufacturers' Association, the British Agrochemical Association, the Agricultural Engineers Association, and many others.

There are dozens of such interest groups monitoring developments which affect their sector of the market, organising meetings, advertising, putting out press releases and lobbying government in their attempts to achieve policies favourable to their members' activities.

The tangled appearance of these industry-linked groups is matched by the consumer organisations, of which there are also dozens. They can be split into a few large and wide-ranging bodies with claims to a representative nature, and many smaller, often single-issue, pressure groups. Among the former are mainstream consumer organisations like the National Consumer Council (NCC), the Consumers in the European Community Group (CECG) or the Consumers Association (CA). They argue that in food policy consumers come first.

Thus in June 1988 the NCC published *Food Policy and the Consumer* which said: 'Consumer organisations have an important role to play in food policy. Their objectives are twofold. First they are in the business of seeing that consumers have the right information to make up their minds sensibly on what they are buying. To this end, consumer organisations lobby for such information as ingredient listing and comprehensive nutrition labelling. Many also publish information about food and related food issues for their members and for consumers generally.

'The second objective is to ensure that the state makes adequate provision for safeguarding the standards and ensuring the safety of the food supply, since consumers cannot make these decisions for themselves. Food technology is advancing daily and the achievement of this second objective places a considerable burden on consumer organisations in terms of the range of interest, knowledge and opinion they must have . . .

'Consumer organisations also have to recognise that they will often be weak in relation to other pressures on the decision-making process for a variety of reasons, mainly that they have much more limited resources than the farming or industry lobbies. With restricted budgets and small executive staff, they have to co-ordinate grass-roots opinion, obtain background information and exert opinion and, on occasions, undertake their own research to formulate a "consumer" view.'

To strengthen them in these tasks, the NCC recommends changes in policy making to give consumers a greater say. They want stronger consumer representation on government committees concerned with advice, policy, and priorities and strategy on food policy. They want much greater openness in these committees; and they want 'consumer impact statements' attached to any proposals which the committees make to ministers. In the 18 months since they published this report, they have gained a form of representation with the establishment of the consumer panel to MAFF's Food Safety Directorate.

Major and wide-ranging, but not necessarily representative, environmental pressure groups like Friends of the Earth (FoE) and Greenpeace also join the food debate. FoE for example monitors pesticide residues in food and pollution in streams and ground-water as well as the habitat changes which come from modern farming technology.

Then there are the more narrowly focussed or single-issue pressure groups such as Compassion in World Farming, the Universities Federation for Animal Welfare, the Food Additives Campaign Team (FACT), the London Food Commission (LFC) and many others. Like the so-called think-tanks discussed above, they may be mainly research-based or more openly political. Often on the opposite wing to organisations like the Adam Smith Institute, such ginger groups campaign to influence food policy directly and indirectly. Political and media contacts are both important, for media attention is a potent influence in raising public concern about food to alter social, political and commercial attitudes.

The LFC has achieved most success in this. It was set up with money from Ken Livingstone's Greater London Council to 'undertake research, evaluate studies and compile information concerning nutrition, diet, health, food production, food distribution, retailing, catering, cooking and consumption and to make available the useful results of such research, studies and information.' Membership is limited to Trade Unions and organisations nominated by them, public bodies such as local authorities and both governmental and QANGO organisations, and voluntary associations and consumer groups. Associate membership is open to people who live or work in Greater London and support its objectives.

The LFC is closely caught up in the adversarial party politics of the food debate. This involvement was marked in May 1989 by an Early Day Motion from Conservative MPs which said 'That this House deplores the activities of the London Food Commission, a registered charity, which has spread panic among consumers about the safety of food and aroused unwarranted fears and suspicions about the activities of the food and pharmaceutical industries; questions whether it's compatible with its charitable status; and congratulates the Minister of Agriculture for his resolute insistence on protecting consumers by acting only on the best scientific evidence in matters of food safety and in the development of new agricultural and veterinary products for use in food production.'

Labour MPs proposed an amendment that 'commends the London Food Commission on its diligent attention to the interests of the British consumer, particularly in relation to the wholesomeness of food, the standards of hygiene in its production, preparation, distribution, storage and retail and the causes of incidence of food posioning; and exhorts all honourable Members seeking to improve the quality of life and the health of the British electorate to heed with great care the cautions and conclusions of this most responsible body . . . and congratulates the former Greater London Council for establishing it.'

This clash, implicit in the policy struggles which increasingly control the food debate, was also stimulated by the publicity surrounding the four-day jamboree in Hyde Park – a kind of Royal Show in central London – which was the centrepiece of the Year of Food and Farming. Critics of the modern food and farming industries which the Year existed to project were inspired by such events to raise their voices. They did so to such effect that, at the end of that May, the *Daily Telegraph* consumer correspondent Virginia Matthews reported that farmers and food manufacturers had been told to hit back at a scare campaign against them by Left-wing activists.

Matthews wrote: 'At a House of Commons meeting, Mrs Teresa Gorman, Conservative MP for Billericay, advised retailing and food industry representatives to go on the offensive.

'Her remarks, for which she claims widespread backbench support, singled out the London Food Commission and Prof Richard Lacey, a Leeds microbiologist, for particular criticism.

'In a document circulated at the meeting, . . . Mrs Gorman spoke of "a series of apparently-unconnected publicity campaigns against preservatives, additives, hormones, salmonella, listeria and cook-chill, which have left the food industry reeling".

'The document adds: "Many of these attacks can be traced back to the London Food Commission . . . little more than a team of Left-wing activists, blessed with a substantial sum from the Greater London Council before it was scrapped".'

Virginia Matthews quoted the Retail Consortium, the Food and Drink Federation and the Institute of Food Science and Technology as more or less cautiously condoning Mrs Gorman's remarks. Professor Will Waites, the food microbiologist who chairs the Food Safety Advisory Service set up by six leading supermarket chains, she quoted as saying: 'The food industry may well feel that it has been unfairly attacked, but there is great oversensitivity.'

Tim Lang, former director of the LFC, has said that both left and right in politics have treated food and health issues with contempt. Certainly, decades of all-party agreement on food have now broken down – perhaps inevitably given the separation between a chablis and sole and a beer and beans approach to dinner – or tea. Groups from both right and left are getting their teeth into food issues and the blood has flowed in consequence.

In the process some striking fellow-feeders have emerged. The Pamela Stephenson-inspired Parents for Safe Food, which includes a group of actresses who have used their publicity value to give an entirely new slant to the old notion of bread and circuses, has been supported by the LFC and in the spring of 1989 appointed Dr Lang as its first director.

The Centre for Policy Studies finds itself arguing a similar case to the Dairy Trades' Federation, which is to urge the attractions of Social Darwinism down on the dairy farm. These alliances will proliferate as they extend links into Europe and America. We have reached a point where in the demonology of the right the LFC and its allies are identified with factions described incongruously as food fascists or Leninists, in the demonology of the left MAFF and the food industry are leeches bleeding consumers for profit. Both distortions add to the anxiety of the woman on the Clapham omnibus, especially when she has not realised how fiercely political hyperbole has peppered the debate. Nor is she helped by media treatment of food issues which has reacted enthusiastically both to the party political and showbiz stimuli.

These battles are now being fought in all developed countries. In Europe, Germans especially but also Dutch and Scandinavians have joined the fray. Although nowhere in the EEC is immune, Catholic countries seem to be innoculated against the worst excesses. The results have been both good and bad.

Good has been the much greater interest and attention paid to food and health and the changes already happening as a result. As one example, mainstream consumer organisations, previously patronised, have become steadily more influential as government and industry have accepted the importance of direct consumer involvement.

Bad has been the Clayton syndrome, the anxiety and resentment stirred by uncertain or contradictory claims which have accompanied so many food scares. Bad too has been the confusion and waste. False scares are manipulated by interest groups and resources are mispent in consequence. Oxford University's Richard Peto has described what can happen with cancer scares. 'Any researcher wants positive results. A lot of the cancer charities rely on money for research. They have PR offices and their job is to exaggerate. Then the journalists report it. There's an increase in hype at each stage.' Fear helps fund-raising but the cash may then be spent on trivial activities. Peto says unequivocally: 'There's a hell of a lot of junk coming out under the guise of epidemiology.' This junk obstructs the debate about nutrition, health and resource management.

More recently, the arrival of genetic engineering as a practical technology has widened the argument. Rifkin's Washington-based Foundation on Economic Trends hoped 'to encourage the exploration and development of alternative and sustainable approaches to urgent human needs including food production, medicine and health care and international security.' It was joined on this side of the Atlantic by German organisations whose opposition to genetic engineering is meshed with appalling memories of the eugenic experiments and doctrines of the Nazis and is so strong that German industry is increasingly reconciled to siting its biotechnical laboratories and factories outside national boundaries. Chief among them is the Gen-ethische Netzwerk (Gen-ethic Network) which has more limited aims than Rifkin's Foundation, namely to gather, assess and disseminate data on genetic engineering with an emphasis on critical perspectives and information, and to organise seminars, conferences and research on the subject. As its name implies, it is also concerned with legal and ethical issues. It has criticised the fact that 'crucial decisions which will determine the course of this technology's development are being made today under immense pressure from industry and governments, who see in it the key to economic power in the future. The broader public interest has been woefully under-represented in this process, if at all, resulting in a dangerous, undemocratic, premature and uncritical promotion of genetic engineering.'

Rifkin's Foundation and the Gen-ethic Network concern themselves with the whole field of biotechnology and collaborate in their opposition to it. Both organisations want to retard or halt the progress of biotechnology at least for long enough for the issues to be thoroughly disentangled. Both can assume a messianic air, with Rifkin in particular a convinced believer that biotechnology will undermine the sacredness of life – and quite determined to forestall this danger. Other groups like Friends of the Earth, Compassion in World Farming or the LFC have joined them in the biotechnology debate, so that extended alliances of lobbyists and interest groups contend in the various areas of medicine, agriculture and wider environmental management.

The clash so far has been most dramatic over BST. The motives behind this opposition have ranged from concerns about animal welfare to worries that a tidal wave of milk might swamp small dairy farmers, and from deeply-felt uncertainties about the overall control of biotechnology to outright opposition, on grounds religious, moral or simply paranoid, to everything to do with genetic engineering. The more this debate has polarised politically, the harder it has been to take an all-round view. Only the mainline consumer organisations, it seemed, looked objectively at the evidence, balanced risks and benefits and accepted that BST could have a useful part to play in modern milk production.

CHAPTER NINE:
The Struggle for Better Regulation

Food regulation – especially, the regulation of food safety – works better in America than in Britain. Their diet may be no better than ours and many think it worse; there is as much conflict about nutrition policy; and there is growing concern about food poisoning. But there is more tolerance of criticism, so that pressure groups and consumers in general feel their views count. This contrasts with British tradition where nanny, who knows what's good for you, either ignores criticism or gives it a clip round the ear.

This is, perhaps, beginning to change. The urges to government secrecy and commercial deregulation, characteristic of Mrs Thatcher's government, went into reverse for food when the first part of the *Report on the Microbiological Safety of Food* was published in mid-February 1990. They had gone slow ahead before that because Sir Mark Richmond, chairman of the committee, had been in close consultation with the Ministry of Agriculture (MAFF) about the contents of the Food Safety Bill.

Richmond recommended greater openness and tighter regulation, and the government accepted both. If it is as good as its word, some at least of Richard North's complaints about secrecy will be met, and to the more frequent publication of data will be added better reporting systems including a national microbiological surveillance and assessment system, and better recording by food producers and retailers to allow consignments of food to be traced to source. But the Campaign for Freedom of Information has expressed fears that disclosure of dangers will still be unnecessarily suppressed.

As for regulation, industry has increasingly grown accustomed to a world where *Guidelines for the Hygienic Manufacture, Distribution and Retail Sale of Sprouted Seeds with Particular Reference to Mung Beans* have become part of the stock-in-trade of management. Now, such detailed guidance will multiply. Part 1 of Richmond endorsed or recommended much more of the same for broiler chicken output, and concluded that 'this represents as comprehensive an approach to the salmonella problem as has – as far as we are aware – been adopted anywhere in the world.' Part 2, due by late summer, proposes to look as closely at eggs, milk and dairy products, fish and shellfish, and red meat, as well as food retailing, food catering and food in the home.

There are important consequences for British farmers. Richmond 'trusts that as a minimum the action already taken by the UK will be used as a model for Community action, especially in the key areas of zoonoses (diseases common to humans and animals) control and the handling and processing of dried protein.' Whether that trust is justified, small farmers here will be increasingly hard put to run businesses which face extra management skills and extra costs to meet the regulations. If European farmers escape more lightly, British consumers will meet more problems like salmonella in Dutch eggs as less-regulated foods are imported.

Other small food businesses face similar problems. 'We are concerned that there is currently little control over the operation of food businesses and that any individual can, without training, open almost any type of food business and start trading.' Richmond recommended that all food businesses should be licensed, but the government rejected this as too restrictive.

The Food Safety Bill which will be passed during the current parliamentary session confirms in principle these moves to tighter regulation. It aims to make sure that modern food technology produces and distributes safe food. It will fail either if it cannot do this or if it cannot persuade consumers it has succeeded.

The omens are mixed. The MAFF's view of the Bill is that of the experienced mechanic tuning up a long-running but reliable engine. The old bus is going well enough with tens of thousands of miles left in her, but a touch here, a twist there and she'll go that much better. The two principles on which this fine-tuning is to be based are freedom of choice and consumer safety. One civil servant said the Bill would adapt, modify, improve and anticipate. It didn't sound like a rebore, much less a replacement engine. This attitude dismays those who want not just a new bus but a whole new transport system – something like the Civil Aviation Authority (CAA), say, adapted to food.

The scope for disagreement remains wide as even one example, that of the temperature chain, shows. Much modern technology relies on keeping processed food at the right temperature from factory to lorry to store to lorry to shop to car to fridge to table. At any link which warms up, microbes can build up. But if the idea of keeping food at the right temperature is simple, the consequences are not. Thus the rate of multiplication of listeria depends, among other things, on the amount present in the first place, temperature, acidity and saltiness of the food, and the length of time before it is eaten. There is room for dispute about the facts, inevitably sharpened by the costs: one degree less for temperature puts millions on refrigeration costs throughout the food chain. Manufacturers and retailers will be immediately concerned and, since consumers will pay in the end, they also will want to be sure that the margin of safety is adequate not old-maidish, and control is enforced not flouted.

The Bill will tighten the links in the chain. Controls over factory practice and hygiene, training of food handlers, registration and where necessary licensing of premises, greater control of unfit food and the strengthening of the enforcement authorities, and control over the introduction of new foods and new processes are all included. These will be secured through enabling powers, and detailed regulations will follow as needed and as Brussels sprouts further directives.

The need for these controls is widely accepted. They have been attacked for not going far enough. Much of industry would, like Richmond, prefer the stricter regulation of licensing rather than registration of premises; consumer groups want legal responsibilities for safety extended to all in the food chain, including farmers; inadequate funding for the local authority workers may undermine inspection and other controls; and all those who want a separate regulatory agency are disappointed. Thus the passage from Bill to Act will be marked by full-scale adversarial politics. The government will maintain its garage mechanic outlook while the opposition will press for complete retooling. The consequences of this on consumers will be complicated by the arrival of the Food Safety Directorate, MAFF's answer to the calls for an independent body to restore public faith in our food supply and the clearest possible case of a pudding whose proof will be in the eating.

Two long-running problems could dish the Directorate. The first is the uneasy fit between the responsibilities of MAFF and the DoH. The division sees MAFF in charge of the food supply and DoH of human illness. Food hygiene, which crosses these arbitrary boundaries, is under the DoH. Thus food safety is uncomfortably stretched between two government departments, and while the civil servants say they will co-operate closely, the eggs' saga shows how easily confusion can arise.

The second is secrecy. There is to be a consumer panel, with direct access to policy makers, whose task will be to review food quality and safety. It will be made up of representatives put forward by consumer groups including the NCC, the Consumers' Association (CA) and the Consumers in the European Community Group (CECG). Will it be a guide dog or a poodle?

Past experience is not happy. Thus Peggy Fenner, when a MAFF junior Minister in 1986, said in the House of Commons: 'Members of the Food Advisory Committee (FAC) are told on appointment that where appropriate they must observe the confidentiality of information passed to them as part of their duties on that Committee. It is the Official Secrets Act that makes it an offence to disclose such information without authority.' Members are not required to sign that Act, and the confidentiality largely concerns commercially-privileged information. But that is not the end of the story. Although the FAC is the MAFF's major advisory committee on food policy there are limits on its access to submissions or reports from other MAFF advisory committees, while because of the split referred to earlier some of the relevant committees – the Committee on Toxicology (COT) or on the Medical Aspects of Food (COMA), for example – are DoH committees in any case.

There are thus considerable restrictions on freedom of action in these advisory committees, and the consumer panel is likely to be caught in similar coils. It will be able to raise issues, rather than working to a MAFF agenda, but access to information from other advisory committees may, like the FAC's, be limited. Worse, important consumer issues such as chill temperatures through the food chain, or the training of food handlers, come under DoH and may thus be excluded from discussion by the panel.

Further, though members of the panel will not be barred from telling journalists what they've been talking about, that freedom to tell is in itself likely to restrict the amount of information available from other committees.

Already, ministers have knocked back some of the representatives put forward by the consumer groups involved on the grounds that they are not 'ordinary' consumers. Since it is not easy to know what an extraordinary consumer might be in this context, the rejections make clear that MAFF doesn't want outside experts making life hard for its inside experts.

Other difficulties arise from the opposite end of the political spectrum. Radical pressure groups have criticised NCC, CA and CECG for dining with the devil, arguing that MAFF will shroud them in a smoke of self-importance and confidentiality and that consumer concerns will suffer in consequence. This refusal to try, much less accept, a role for direct consumer contribution is a clear instance of the distortions imposed by head-butting habits of mind.

So the panel may be dished both by internal restrictions and external criticisms. If so, the Food Safety Directorate will be another burnt offering with hot political implications. A survey by Diagnostics in the autumn of 1989 showed that while 9% of the sample trusted what the government said about food, 60% no longer did. The same survey showed that three out of four of us are so muddled about food safety we no longer know who to trust. Given that lack of trust, it will do the government little good to achieve food safety if it is not clearly seen to be achieved.

The NCC has made some telling points about all this in a recent survey of US practice. It said: 'In the UK, critics are seen, at best, as a minor nuisance which has to be tolerated or, at worst, as some breed of dangerous food activists who are to be silenced and excluded at all costs. In the US, critics are regarded as a group of people who probably have something useful to contribute to the debate, particularly in the area of food safety, where there is much public concern. We could detect none of the hostile, confrontational attitudes which have done so much to damage relationships between industry, producers, consumers and regulators in the UK.'

The structure of food regulation is in many ways similar in both countries. Here it is split between MAFF and DoH, there between the United States Department of Agriculture (USDA) and the Department of Health and Human Services (DHHS), with the Environmental Protection Agency (EPA) also joining in. In both countries the agriculture ministries are responsible for maintaining the health of domestic farming; in America the Food and Drugs Administration is part of the DHHS whereas the new British Food Safety Directorate will be part of MAFF.

Some of the details are also similar: the recently-established US Advisory Committee on Microbiological Criteria for Foods which is looking at policies to prevent food poisoning is paralleled by the UK Committee on Microbiological Food Safety. But the US Committee includes consumer representation, publishes its agenda in advance, holds open meetings and publishes its minutes, while – apart from the inclusion of one consumer representative – none of these things happens with the UK committee.

Based on its experience of UK and US food regulation, the NCC has recommended changes. These should include:

- separation of food regulation from the department which controls and promotes the food and farming industries

- all food safety concerns to become the responsibility of a single independent agency
- this agency to contain a strong consumer affairs department
- to be open and accountable to the public
- to be able to co-ordinate closely with other related agencies – to set nutrition and public health targets which link food safety, standards, science and surveillance.

The NCC argues: 'The creation of a separate regulatory office would give consumers far greater confidence in the independent nature and adequacy of the consumer protection perspective in the field of food safety, food standards and nutrition. It would also provide a firmer and more effective basis for the continued development of a dynamic UK food industry. It is essential for industry to be able to rely on an open and respected regulatory system. One of the most damaging aspects of the current situation is the suspicion, however mistaken or misinformed, of the secret and close relationship between the food industry and government, which has been to the benefit of no one and which threatens to jeopardise some of the innovative developments in the UK food industry.

'We also recommend that the office should have a division of consumer affairs which would be responsible for ensuring that consumers participate in decision-making and that they receive appropriate information and education about food safety and new developements in food technology. A worrying aspect of the current UK situation is the gap between scientific knowledge and public perception. This situation needs to be addressed urgently.'

If the government gets the Food Safety Bill wrong, changes like this will come to the top of the food politics agenda. At the same time, consumers will turn more to Brussels, especially as the Single Market approaches. Much of the legislation surrounding 1992 is anyway about food, animal and plant hygiene and will have to be incorporated into British law. A whole new battleground is rapidly building within the EC on these issues. Indeed the Commission, backed by the European Parliament, is moving towards an FDA-type of regulatory agency, similar to that proposed by the NCC above, to control food safety and food law. Should this happen, UK laws will have to harmonise.

There are, however, endless confounding issues. One example is labelling. The EEC at first said that, so long as consumers get proper information on what's in what they eat, the nature and composition of foodstuffs need not be defined by law except where safety and public health are involved. So a sausage need not contain a minimum proportion of meat, but the label would have to say precisely how much meat it did contain, and anything thus labelled which can be legally sold in one member state could be sold in all.

The Commission does not want to place in a 'legislative straitjacket the culinary riches of European countries.'

The French have become uneasy about this. They have seen Brie go the same way as Cheddar – that is, become the name for a cheese which may be made anywhere rather than in the particular place where it originated – and fear that other gallic gourmet goodies may follow. They argue for quality provisions which would define what's in different foods made where so that an Ardennes paté or Toulouse sausage could not come from Melton Mowbray or Cumberland.

These and other arguments have persuaded Brussels that nutritional information will only be compulsory where foods make a specific nutritional claim like high fibre or low in saturated fats. For other foods, such information will be voluntary. So long as these limited demands are met, governments cannot keep out imports which comply with them. The battle for better labelling will go on, with the compulsory use of full nutritional labels a constant, but still distant, goal.

While national and international controls may alter attitudes slowly, and the Food Safety Bill will affect the credibility of MAFF more quickly, consumer attitudes will continue to have the biggest influence on food supply. Close to one in three consumers buys with a green tinge now, and no industry can ignore numbers like that. If by the 1970s Sainsbury knew that too many manufacturers spent R&D cash on new technology processes rather than on new products – and hence produced more processed foods and not enough fresh ones – other major retailers also spotted that trend and moved to meet it, first through more frozen and chilled products, then through menu dishes, expanding fruit, vegetable and fresh meat sales and then through prepacked salads and other con- venience fresh foods. Now, over one-third of the £33 billion spent on all food goes on chilled and frozen food, and fresh fruit and vegetables are a growing market sector.

Manufacturers were also driven to follow technolo- gies which kept food 'fresh' longer. As well as chilling, heating is important, with high temperature short time processing, and multitherm processing offering two long- life possibilities. Controlled atmosphere packaging is another approach. So are seed-based biotechnologies which alter enzyme production in harvested crops to slow ripening and spoilage. Irradiation is a further option. Any or all of them would help lessen both spoilage and the yearly increases in food poisoning which have disfig- ured the last two decades – but acceptance of these techniques by consumers will govern their uptake.

One way or another, however, convenience and reliability will remain important selling points. They will go on stimulating new technologies which in turn will provoke new fears and uncertainties, so food scares will not go away. But a better understanding of the risks and benefits, to the environment as well as to ourselves, will slowly be achieved as James Lovelock's message about getting the food industry to synthesise all our food in order to take the strain off Gaia spreads to reach a wider audience.